Generating Savings for Latin American Development

Edited by
Robert Grosse

The publisher of this book is the North-South Center Press at the University of Miami.

The mission of the North-South Center is to promote better relations and serve as a catalyst for change among the United States, Canada, and the nations of Latin America and the Caribbean by advancing knowledge and understanding of the major political, social, economic, and cultural issues affecting the nations and peoples of the Western Hemisphere.

All copyright inquiries should be addressed to the publisher: North-South Center Press, 1500 Monza Avenue, Coral Gables, Florida 33146-3027, U.S.A., phone 305-284-8914, fax 305-284-5089, or e-mail mvega@nsc.msmail.miami.edu.

To order or to return books, contact Lynne Rienner Publishers, Inc., 1800 30th Street, Suite 314, Boulder, CO 80301-1026, 303-444-6684, fax 303-444-0824.

Library of Congress Cataloging-in-Publication Data

Generating savings for Latin American development: a project of the North-South Center / edited by Robert Grosse.
     p. cm.
     Includes bibliographical references (p.) and index.

ISBN 1-57454-044-0 (alk. paper: pbk.)

     1. Savings and investment—Latin America. 2. Investments, Foreign—Latin America. 3. Finance—Latin America. 4. Latin America—Economic conditions—1982– I. Grosse, Robert E. II. University of Miami. North-South Center.
HC130.S3G46 1997
339.4'3'098—dc21   97-21496
                                                                                                            CIP

Printed in the United States of America/TS

02 01 00 99 98 97   6 5 4 3 2 1

Contents

Preface

This project is a continuation of the work initiated by Robert Grosse under the auspices of the External Debt Program of the North-South Center at the University of Miami. Previous stages of the program have included the project entitled *Private Sector Solutions to the Latin American Debt Problem,* which comprised 10 papers by leading authors on international finance. Papers ranged from analysis of the Bolivian debt restructuring agreement of 1985 to a comparison of debt restructuring instruments, such as debt-equity swaps and bond issues, to a view of capital market development in Latin America. That project led to a conference in Miami during June 1991 and subsequent publication of the papers as a book by the same title (North-South Center 1992). Two of the papers also were published as articles in the *Journal of Interamerican Studies and World Affairs,* and three of the papers were published as *Discussion Papers* by the International Business Center at the University of Miami.

From the first stage, in addition to the direct conclusions produced by the analyses, two key areas were identified for further research. Based on the analysis by Ravi Ramamurti, it was determined that privatization of state-owned companies was a potentially key means of pulling investment into the region from foreign as well as domestic investors (including those with wealth held overseas). Ramamurti then led another North-South Center project that focused on privatization, specifically in the airlines and telecommunications sectors. This project also produced 10 papers, all of which were published in 1996 as a book entitled *Privatizing Monopolies: Lessons from the Telecommunications and Transport Sectors in Latin America* (The Johns Hopkins University Press). One of the papers by Ramamurti on privatization of telecommunications in Mexico was published by the North-South Center as an *Agenda Paper* in 1994, entitled *Telephone Privatization in a Large Country: Mexico.*

Another key point that emerged from analysis during the first stage of the program was that governments, although not the initiators of innovative solutions to the debt crisis, were integral participants in resolving that crisis. Since performance has varied so widely across the region, it was decided to pursue a second stage aimed at comparing these government responses. Grosse then led a second project in the debt program, focused on government responses to the debt problem. Seven papers were generated during this stage from six countries that discussed their governments' policies for dealing with the external debt burden during the 1980s and early

1990s. A conference was held in Miami in January 1994 to present these papers, which subsequently were published in 1995 by the North-South Center Press as a book, entitled *Government Responses to the Latin American Debt Problem*. Three of the papers were published as *Discussion Papers* of the University of Miami International Business Center.

At present, the crisis aspects of the external debt problem in Latin America have been resolved (for example, see Grosse's *The End of the Latin American Debt Crisis? Issues* paper published by the North-South Center in November 1992). The fundamental issue that remains is to identify and understand the sources and means of financing economic development in Latin America in the future. While foreign commercial bank debt may not be the primary source of external funding it was in the 1970s and 1980s, it still will play a major role in this process. Equity investment from both foreign and domestic sources has become a much larger source of finance in the 1990s. Bond issues have become once again a major source of external finance. And, very importantly, domestic capital markets have developed rapidly in the past few years, such that they too serve as channels of funds to borrowers in Latin American countries.

Based on this background, the North-South Center has continued its research on Latin American financing issues by sponsoring a project entitled *Generating Savings for Latin American Development*, which was begun in 1994 and concludes with the publication of this book.

The authors and general editor would like to thank Ambler H. Moss, Jr., Director of the North-South Center, for his unfailing support of the debt program and the various staff members of the Center and the North-South Center Press who have worked to help make this a successful project and publication.

Chapter 1

Introduction

Robert Grosse

L atin American economies have ridden a rollercoaster of economic
development during the past 20 years. From the high-growth, relatively
low-inflation period of the late 1970s and beginning of the 1980s, the region
then plunged into a protracted debt and growth crisis that lasted through
the 1980s. In 1989, major economic policy shifts began to occur throughout
Latin America, predominantly in favor of open-market economics and away
from the previous two decades of largely inward-looking economic
development policies. These shifts came in response to the severely
depressed conditions that had accompanied the debt crisis, and they were
strongly encouraged by international lenders from both public and private
sectors. Changes in Latin American economic policies were accompanied
by global economic policy shifts (especially following the fall of the Berlin
Wall) toward open markets. This phenomenon reinforced the Latin
American path, because Eastern European countries also were competing
for foreign investment and lending resources. Latin American countries had
to respond competitively or lose out on some of the external financial
resources. The combination of these various conditions and policies has
resulted in a new period of strong growth with generally low inflation in
Latin America during the 1990s.

Of course, development analysts and government policymakers
would like to understand how to smooth out the dramatic business and debt
cycles and to define a path of sustainable, low-inflation growth. No single
plan appears likely to fit all cases, but there are some parts of the policy
puzzle that seem reasonably appropriate across the board. For example,
reducing the size of the public sector and allowing more economic activity
to be carried out by private firms — deregulated in general but regulated
to avoid monopolistic practices — are widely agreed to be viable policy
planks.[1] Similarly, reducing import barriers and allowing greater regional
and global freedom of trade activity are helpful and not particularly
controversial policy positions at this time.

The volatility that has hindered Latin American economic growth
came not only in the form of business cycles and debt cycles but also in
government policy variability. That is, governments have been notorious for
changing the rules of the game on business and especially on financial

issues during the past several decades in Latin America. Policy regimes have not been exactly cyclical but rather subject to major and unanticipated change. Stabilization of the policy regime itself is a means for aiding business growth, and this has become a reality throughout much of the region in the 1990s.

Another part of the macroeconomic context is the relationship among savings, investment, and national income. For one thing, savings is a stabilizing factor on consumption. That is, even as income and consumption vary over business cycles and periods of economic instability, current and previous savings can be used to smooth consumption patterns and thus provide some degree of economic stability.

It appears clear that foreign savings, mobilized in the form of direct and portfolio investment, is a useful tool to build capital investment in the region. Analogously, domestic savings should be used to build local capital investment, although there has been a strong downturn in domestic savings in several of the countries of the region, with no obvious connection to the growth of capital formation. Overall, of course, domestic and foreign savings are the only sources for capital formation; so, in an accounting sense, this is tautological.

The analytical questions are these: How does savings contribute to the process of capital formation in Latin America? How does domestic savings relate to domestic investment? Moreover, how does foreign investment relate to both Latin American savings and capital investment in the region? The project at hand tries to answer these questions. The underlying question posed by all the authors was how can savings be generated and mobilized to support economic development in Latin America. In the chapters that constitute this book, the broad question is divided into smaller parts and analyzed in detail for the region and for several individual countries.

The specific analyses that constitute this project are six research papers covering selected topics that are described below, all of which relate to the sources of financing that can fund the growth and development of Latin American economies and the mechanisms that can channel these savings into productive investment.

The first study, by Evan Tanner, discusses the pattern of savings in Latin America during the 1980s and the early 1990s. He demonstrates that, despite the huge turnaround in investment that has taken place in the region since the end of the debt crisis in approximately 1989, there is a decline in the savings rate in most countries of the region during this period. The explanation for such a negative relationship between savings and investment is not transparent. For policymakers, such an observation poses a puzzle. Tanner uses his paper to analyze this situation and to explain the reasons why savings have not moved with investment in Latin America.

His analysis explores the relationships between savings and future output, between public and private savings, and between savings and consumption. The intent is to identify key factors that contribute to determining national savings and to clarify their relationship to savings.

Each of these tasks is undertaken in light of the finding that national savings rates have fallen in many countries of Latin America during the past decade.

In his paper, Tanner draws on some traditional ideas in economics to address the savings/output puzzle. Among such traditional ideas is Milton Friedman's permanent income hypothesis. This relationship, between savings and future income, poses the hypothesis that savings may fall due to anticipation of higher future income. According to the permanent income hypothesis, rational consumers should consume more today and reduce current savings if they expect a rise in future income. Using an econometric model carefully linked to optimizing consumer behavior, Tanner is able to show that Latin American consumers have demonstrated "forward-looking behavior"; that is, they have adjusted their savings patterns in anticipation of future income movements. This is consistent with the permanent income hypothesis, and it suggests that a decreased savings rate in Latin America may be due to expectations of increased future incomes in the region.

Next, looking at the relationship between public sector and private savings, Tanner explores the possible substitutability between the two. Perhaps private sector savings rates have declined because the government sector has improved its savings behavior. In other words, perhaps government savings crowds out private savings, as government consumption often is found to crowd out private consumption. Statistical tests demonstrate that government and private savings in Latin America for the 1980-1992 period almost completely substitute for one another. An increase in government savings as a percentage of gross domestic product (GDP) was offset considerably by a decline in private savings, with estimates ranging from 50 to 90 percent, depending on the exact form of the estimating equation. This finding would help explain the decline in Latin American savings, if the government savings rate increases during the period (as it did).

Finally, Tanner considers the relationship between government savings and aggregate consumption. His assertion is that an increase in government spending would produce a decrease in overall consumption (and possibly an increase in private savings). This relationship does seem to hold, and thus a persistent decrease in government spending, as is underway with the programs of privatization and government budget responsibility throughout Latin America, may produce a decrease in private savings along with an increase in private consumption.

The basic conclusion of Tanner's empirical investigation is that there are several macroeconomic factors that may be contributing to Latin America's decline in savings during the past decade. Expectations of future improvements in income may lead consumers to save less today. Increased government savings due to better budget management may result in reduced private savings, since the two are apparently substitutes. Looking at the same issue from a slightly different perspective, if government spending declines, then it may spur private spending and also lead to reduced private savings. Altogether, this paints a very interesting picture of the macroeconomies of Latin America with respect to the savings issue.

The analysis then moves to consider the broad array of long-term financing sources that are available to Latin America in the 1990s. The first discussion of savings and other macroeconomic aggregates such as consumption and government spending focused on domestic sources of income and wealth that could be harnessed to contribute to economic growth. Now the perspective is widened to include foreign sources of savings that likewise may contribute to capital formation and growth.

Clarice Pechman examines the range of sources of long-term finance available to Latin American borrowers. Her focus is particularly on the experience of Brazil, the largest Latin American country and one where problems of hyperinflation and other severe macroeconomic instability have been prevalent during the past 15 years.

Pechman chronicles the sources of savings that supported capital formation in Brazil since 1970. During the debt crisis years of the 1980s, domestic government savings were negative (that is, the government ran a budget deficit). Private savings increased somewhat at the beginning of that period, but the result of the government's dissaving was a reduction in capital formation. Foreign savings contributed about one-quarter of the total, and that also declined with the onset of the debt crisis. Interestingly, the paths of domestic savings and foreign savings in Brazil tended to move in opposite directions, with domestic savings tending to rise in periods of economic downturn and vice versa.

Looking more specifically at instruments used by companies to obtain financial resources, the paper identifies a wide range of alternatives. Debenture bonds have been one major source of funding since the early 1980s. Short-term commercial paper also has become an important additional source of funding since the end of the debt crisis. In just the past two years, Brazilian firms have been permitted to issue depository receipts abroad, and this instrument has been used to raise more than US$1 billion in each of those years (compared with less than US$500 million in commercial paper issues and a similar value of debentures). Bank financing has dwarfed these sources during the same period. Domestic bank lending for export finance alone has provided over US$30 billion during each of the past five years. The range of financing instruments is quite large, and Pechman's paper describes characteristics and funding levels under each of the instruments.

The paper then looks at Brazil's economic stabilization programs of the 1990s and discusses the impacts of these programs on the country's ability to attract and maintain foreign financing. The most recent Real plan has managed to reduce inflation well below 100 percent per year and may even lead to single-digit price increases in the late 1990s. This successful stabilization, if maintained, very likely will attract more capital investment in Brazil from both domestic and foreign sources. Pechman notes the exposure of Brazil to foreign short-term capital investments, which can be withdrawn very quickly during times of economic uncertainty or crisis. This problem can only be reduced through continued demonstration of policy stability, and the most appropriate government policy is to establish rules that attract long-term foreign investment, particularly in capital projects (foreign direct investment — FDI).

Overall, the savings pattern in Brazil has become less volatile during the mid-1990s. The domestic savings rate has not grown noticeably, but foreign savings coming into the country have grown sharply and have supported the observed faster rate of capital formation. The foreign savings have flowed into Brazil both because of an improving economic outlook and also because of a growing number of financial instruments that permit foreign investors to select among instruments with a wide variety of maturities, risks, and liquidities. Pechman asserts that the Brazilian government needs to continue a consistent, transparent policy toward capital inflows and outflows, as well as a clear policy toward foreign firms that would like to do business in Brazil through foreign direct investment.

These first chapters of the study emphasized the macroeconomic aspects of savings. The next two chapters take a more micro-level view to examine the use of particular financial instruments and institutions for mobilizing savings in Latin America.

Roberto Curci and Fernando Jaramillo focus on the American Depository Receipt (ADR) as a mechanism for attracting foreign savings into Latin American firms. The ADR has existed for many years, but only since the debt crisis of the 1980s has it become a widely used instrument for Latin American borrowers. Curci and Jaramillo describe the instrument, discuss its costs and benefits for Latin American issuers, and present empirical evidence on the use of ADRs by Latin American borrowers in the 1990s.

The paper begins with a detailed commentary on the characteristics of the ADR — a financial derivative based on stock shares issued in a company's home country and then held on deposit by a bank, which consequently issues ADRs denominated in dollars in the U.S. market. ADRs function more or less as U.S. stock issues of the foreign company, but in this form the securities are not subject to the same level of information disclosure and compliance as if the firm issued stock shares directly into the U.S. market. ADRs can even be issued as private placements, with a very low level of information disclosure required, as long as the issue is sold to sophisticated institutional investors.

In the 1990s, ADR issues have been used frequently by emerging market issuers, particularly from Latin America. In 1993, for example, there were more ADR issues by Mexican firms than by firms from any other country. The ADR mechanism has been used successfully in the process of privatization of state-owned enterprises. The Argentine oil company, Yacimientos Petrolíferos Fiscales (YPF), was privatized in 1993 through a global share offering, in which more than US$2 billion of ADRs were sold on the New York Stock Exchange (and approximately US$2 billion more shares and global depository receipts were sold in Buenos Aires and London). Even the smaller countries of Latin America have seen companies successfully launch ADR issues. Colombia currently has eight companies with shares traded as ADRs in the U.S. market.

Curci and Jaramillo discuss the reasons for the low level of participation in the ADR market by Colombian firms, which constitute less than 1 percent of the Latin American ADRs traded. They note that, in addition to company characteristics such as size and profitability, there are country characteristics that play an important role in determining the success or lack of success of ADR issues. The political instability and social violence in Colombia in recent years apparently have contributed to the relatively low number of ADR issues by Colombian firms, although another key factor is the low level of awareness by Colombian firms of the availability of this international financing alternative.

The authors argue that ADRs are likely to grow in importance for Colombian firms, since early results for the first issuers have been very positive in terms of funds generated and performance of the ADRs that satisfies investors. It appears that the next major expansion of ADR issues from Colombian firms will come from the industrial sector, since almost one-half of existing issues were by banks and other financial firms.

Probably the single most important mechanism for channeling domestic savings into capital investment in Latin America for the 1990s and beyond is the pension fund. When Chile moved to privatize pension funds and allow them to invest in a wide range of financial instruments at the beginning of the 1980s, this was the first step in the country's transformation of its financial structure that is still continuing today. The huge improvement in Chilean savings that has followed the pension fund liberalization program is being studied and replicated around the world in the 1990s. This phenomenon is the subject of the next paper.

Erik Haindl analyzes the highly successful Chilean program of pension fund privatization begun in 1980. His paper describes the process usesd by Chile to move from a pension system based on the "pay-as-you-go" principle, in which current wage and salary earners are taxed on their income to pay pensions to people who have already retired. In this system, there is no link between the income earner and pension benefits — at a future time when the income earner retires, he/she is totally dependent on future income earners to pay in enough funds for that future pension. In 1980, Chile switched to a fully funded pension system, in which each income earner maintains a personal pension account and contributes to it. Upon retirement, the individual receives a pension equal to the amount contributed during his/her working life, plus the interest earned during that period.

Haindl demonstrates that the fully funded pension system is superior to the pay-as-you-go system in economic terms, since it does not create incentives for people to circumvent the contribution mechanism today to take advantage of others' contributions in the future. He defines and describes possible various distortions produced by a pay-as-you-go pension system and shows how each is eliminated or mitigated under the fully funded system. For example, individuals may be myopic in believing that their contributions to a pension are totally lost as a tax. Therefore, they will act accordingly, by perhaps reducing their work or moving into the informal, untaxed, sector. Once a fully funded pension system is in operation, each person will see that his/her own pension is conserved for future drawdown, and no transfer takes place that might distort behavior.

A problem that does arise with the fully funded system is the financing of the transition period between pay-as-you-go funding and self-funding. Where do resources come from to pay the pensions of those who retire just after initiation of the new system and before they have time to accumulate pension contributions? Since this problem certainly must be handled by government contribution, the subsequent question is how to obtain the funds — through new taxation or through borrowing. There is no correct answer to this question but rather a set of considerations that favor one or another of the alternatives. One means of funding current pensions during the transition is to raise taxes; this method will cut disposable income and current consumption, but it also may encourage greater savings and investment. Another means of funding current pensions would be to borrow in financial markets. This would, to some extent, crowd out private sector borrowing and thus possibly reduce private sector investment. Haindl argues that such borrowing is likely just to replace existing government borrowing that is being used to fund the pay-as-you-go pension system. This issue is left with a clear definition of the alternatives and an assertion that the government's borrowing strategy is least distortionary because it only justifies the borrowing that, in fact, was occurring under the existing system.

The Chilean government actually funded the transition to a fully funded pension system by cutting government spending, thus reducing benefits to the former beneficiaries of that spending. Government savings actually declined somewhat during the early transition, as public spending cuts on other activities did not fully match increases in government spending on the transition pensions. Private savings dropped strikingly for the first two years during the transition, then rebounded and reached a much higher level than in previous decades.

The government also made the switch to the new pension system voluntary. An individual could choose to continue with the old pension plan or move into the new system. It became clear in the first few years of operation that the fully funded pensions offered higher returns to participants, so participation in the new plan increased from 40 percent of the labor force in 1981 to 94 percent in 1994.

Privatization of the pension system not only meant that the system had moved to the fully funded structure but that private companies were permitted to manage the pension funds. Competition among private sector pension plan management companies began immediately and continues actively today. The funds are permitted to invest only in approved kinds of assets, and they are overseen by regulators to try to protect the system. Basically, it is a private system, and workers may choose to place their pensions with any approved management company and to switch management companies at any time.

This pension management structure has led to pension fund investments that hold approximately 40 percent of government bonds, 12 percent of mortgages, 5 percent of company bonds, and almost 34 percent of stock shares in the Chilean market in 1994. Since 1993, the plans have been allowed to hold a limited percentage of their assets in foreign government securities. Undoubtedly, in Chile, development of the private pension management system has contributed very importantly to the growth and development of the capital market.

After his discussion of the mechanics of the pension system and the costs and benefits involved, Haindl takes up the issue of how pension privatization has affected savings in Chile. He presents a model of domestic savings in Chile and demonstrates how, over the period 1976-1994, savings has risen from approximately 17 percent of GDP to more than 26 percent of GDP. This, in large part, has been the result of the implementation of the new pension system. His regression model shows that approximately 3 percent of GDP is now saved directly in the pension plans. Another 3 percent of GDP is estimated to be saved as a result of the impact of the pension funds on developing a broader and deeper capital market in Chile. In total, almost two-thirds of the growth in savings in Chile is attributable to the switch to the privately managed, fully funded pension plan. Undoubtedly, questions may be posed as to the precise magnitude of this effect. However, taking into account tax changes, shifts in foreign investment, and crowding out of private with government savings, Haindl's model shows a very impressive positive impact of the pension plan switch on aggregate savings in Chile.

How applicable are this model and its results to other Latin American countries? Beyond any doubt, the results are impressive and have encouraged other governments in the region to consider similar moves. Argentina and Peru already have moved to privatize their pension systems, and virtually all other governments in the region are considering or have considered similar moves. This is truly a major success story in Latin American economic history.

Robert Grosse next looks at the patterns of foreign direct investment (FDI) into Latin America during the past two decades. The initial part of his paper describes FDI flows into the region by target country and by industry. Not surprisingly, the largest flows of direct investment almost always have gone into the largest markets, Brazil and Mexico, though in the post-debt crisis period, Argentina has outstripped the more restrictive Brazil in attracting FDI. Direct investment is compared with other sources of foreign finance into Latin America, and, effectively, direct and portfolio investment combined have dominated capital flows into Latin America during the 1990s. This contrasts with the 1970s and 1980s, when bank loans were much greater in value, and the 1950s and 1960s, when government lending was greater, followed by bank loans.

Grosse chooses three basic questions that are answered in subsequent analysis. First, the macro reasons for FDI into Latin America are explored, using factors such as market size, relative rates of return, and country risk to explain the variations of FDI flows by country and over time. Statistical testing shows that market size and per capita income, as well as the local rate of return and the government's fiscal balance, are positively related to FDI flows. In the same modeling effort, the international price of oil and the country's political risk rating were negatively related to FDI flows. All of these results were found in data examined for the 1980s and early 1990s.

A second question concerned the relationship between foreign direct investment and local capital investment. Are they substitutes, complements, or are they unrelated? It appears from casual observation that both domestic and foreign direct investment follow the pattern of confidence in the national economy. When domestic capital investment falls off, usually FDI seems to decline also. Simple statistical testing produces a 90 percent correlation between the two activities, which supports the assertion that FDI and local capital formation are complements of one another rather than substitutes for each other.

A third and final question concerned the relationship between foreign direct investment and local savings. Does foreign direct investment contribute to growth in savings in Latin America? Or alternatively, does an increased savings rate lead to greater FDI into countries that experience such a shift? The answers to both questions were quite striking. In simple statistical tests, there has been virtually no relationship between savings rates and FDI flows into Latin American countries during the past two decades. Domestic savings simply do not correlate with FDI inflows. Casual empiricism likewise shows no indication that foreign firms have been influenced by domestic savings patterns in their decisions to set up plants, offices, or other economic activities in Latin America.

In sum, the relationship of FDI to domestic savings is very limited at best. FDI is much more related to capital formation in Latin American countries — it appears to reinforce domestic capital formation activity. FDI represents a form of external savings that can and does contribute to capital formation and economic growth in Latin America, without having a sustained impact on the savings rate in the region.

Taking another perspective on savings in the region, José M. González-Eiras examines the impact of the process of economic opening in Latin America on aggregate savings and investment. He explores the relationship of savings to national investment throughout the region; then observes whether the process of economic opening has produced any shifts in the levels and trends of aggregate savings and investment.

With respect to the relationship between domestic savings and domestic investment, it appears that a clear de-linking has occurred or has existed during the debt crisis and its aftermath. González-Eiras finds that changes in domestic savings are positively and significantly related to changes in domestic investment, but that investment only adjusts about 20 percent as much as the savings movements (during the period 1975-1993).

This may mean that investment is more responsive to changes in total savings, domestic and foreign, rather than just to domestic savings.

The process of economic opening has taken place in varying degrees, and it began at various times in Latin America. González-Eiras divides the dozen largest countries in the region into subgroups according to when they began the *apertura económica* process. Bolivia, Chile, and Mexico are the longest-term reformers, with major economic openings that began in the mid-1980s (and even earlier in Chile). Costa Rica and Uruguay are grouped in a second category, since their reform processes began in about 1990. Finally, Argentina, Brazil, Colombia, Ecuador, Paraguay, Peru, and Venezuela are grouped as the most recent reformers.

Using this grouping method, González-Eiras tested to see if domestic investment for each group was influenced by domestic savings and by economic opening, defined as the volume of external trade. Statistical results show that domestic investment was an important cause of variations in domestic savings for each group and that the economic opening variable was correctly signed but insignificant in each case. The net result provides weak support for the assertion that economic opening has contributed positively to the growth of savings in Latin America.

A second goal of the paper was to explore the impact of economic opening on the levels of savings and investment in Latin American countries. Again, dividing the countries into groups according to when their opening processes began, González-Eiras finds that the countries that began their economic openings sooner have seen positive shifts in domestic savings between the periods 1980-1985 and 1989-1993. The countries that began their reforms later actually have seen a net decline in their savings rate from the previous decade. Interestingly, in all cases, investment was lower in the more recent period, although this point was not investigated statistically.

Given the small number of years of available data in the period since economic opening, a more detailed statistical analysis was not undertaken in this study. Even with relatively limited data, the analysis was able to establish that there has been a noticeable improvement in the savings rate of countries that began their opening processes sooner — and an expectation that other countries will follow the same path in the next few years. The pattern of investment will be affected positively by this increase in savings, but the overall level of investment depends on other factors, such as foreign savings, which are not analyzed here.

Across all these individual studies, there appears to be a common thread that links Latin American investment to both domestic and foreign savings. This is not surprising in a world of interdependent economies, but it is interesting to see the relationship reconfirmed in the 1980s and 1990s. The lessons to draw from this finding are numerous, from encouraging the continuation of the process of economic opening that attracts foreign capital inflows to building domestic capital markets that allow domestic savings to be mobilized to support investment.

One point that is not emphasized in the analyses is that attraction of foreign capital in the form of portfolio investment, that is, investment in stocks and bonds and other securities, brings with it an inherent risk of disinvestment. When confidence in a country wanes, investors will move their funds to more secure investments, frequently in other countries. This reality of an open international capital market implies that Latin American countries will need to generate confidence in the investing public (domestic and foreign) and maintain it throughout economic cycles if the countries want to avoid massive, destabilizing capital flows. The Mexican crisis of December 1994 is recent enough to punctuate that statement.

How can a country maintain investor confidence? There is no easy answer to this question, when governments must forever follow a balancing act to move forward economically, while at the same time serving social and political interests. The problem is even more complex, since it is unclear how specific economic policies will operate in different countries at different times, so the policy choices themselves are not fully understood or confinable. The answer can only be partial. Investor confidence tends to be maintained when government policies are changed infrequently and transparently. A process of economic policymaking that is observable and logical may be the best answer to this dilemma, since business cycles cannot be eliminated and since international capital flows will be more rather than less volatile as markets become more open. Perhaps the good news is that industrial country portfolio managers, in trying to achieve maximum benefits from diversification, need to increase their holdings of securities from emerging markets. Since Latin American markets constitute a large part of the emerging market total, portfolio diversification into this region is almost guaranteed in the next decade or more as portfolio adjustments are made. This assures the region of availability of foreign savings for investment, so long as the markets remain open to the inflow — and outflow — of that foreign savings.

The following chapters move from a broad view of savings and investment throughout the region to the views of specific countries and financing mechanisms and then back. The goals of this book are to paint a clear picture of the patterns of savings in Latin American countries and to see how foreign savings, or foreign finance, can contribute to building up both savings and investment in the region.

Chapter 2

Savings, Stabilization, and Reform in Latin America: Patterns and Policies in the 1990s

Evan Tanner

Abstract

Recently, many Latin American economies have reduced inflation and implemented major policy reforms. Although these new policies have brought many benefits, savings rates still pose a challenge to policymakers. In some countries, stabilization has caused consumption booms, reducing private and national savings rates. Some tests with pooled data from 18 Latin American countries from 1960 to 1993 suggest several relationships among savings, fiscal policy, and short-run growth. First, savings may fall in anticipation of increased income growth. Tests suggest that lagged savings are correlated negatively and significantly with current increases in income growth. This observation is consistent with forward-looking behavior and the permanent income hypothesis. Second, estimates reveal a negative relationship between private and public savings, indicating a high degree of substitutability between the two. Third, there appears to be a strong negative relationship between government expenditures and private sector consumption. During stabilizations, government expenditures typically fall.

Introduction

The late 1980s and early 1990s have brought much good news for Latin America. Policy reform and stabilization have occurred in much of the region. In contrast with the early 1980s, budget deficits have been slashed, trade regimes liberalized, state enterprises sold, and regulations streamlined. The benefits of reform include lower inflation, higher growth, and increased trade.

Savings rates pose a concern, however. Stabilization in some Latin American countries has caused booms in consumption that have reduced private and national savings rates. Presumably, one of the goals of policy reform should be to increase savings for more investment.[1] Certain basic economic theory, on the other hand, suggests that savings may decrease with successful stabilizations and reforms. For example, according to the permanent income hypothesis, if income is expected to rise in the future, consumption should rise today. Also, cuts in the government budget deficit may decrease private sector savings, if the two are substitutes.[2] As well, a disinflation should reduce the costs of credit intermediation, increasing domestic borrowing and consumption.[3] Finally, variables determined in world markets, such as interest rates, also have an effect on savings.

This chapter examines some recent developments in savings in Latin America. It is based on evidence of savings behavior using pooled data. The cases of three countries that have stabilized recently, Mexico, Argentina, and Peru, are examined. The first section reviews recent patterns of savings in several Latin American countries. In three notable cases, Argentina, Mexico, and Peru, falls in private and national savings have accompanied policy reforms and disinflations. The second section examines the hypothesis that savings responds to expected future changes in output. The third section examines the substitutability of private and public sector savings. The evidence suggests that private and public savings may be close substitutes. The fourth section looks at the effect of fiscal policy on consumption and disinflation, and the fifth section discusses some policy implications. Stabilization packages in several countries have included short-term measures to curb consumption. Measures include high interest rates, credit controls, and taxes on short-term borrowing. What are the justifications of these policies? Do these policies increase welfare? Are they second-best policies for more fundamental reforms? Finally, the sixth section presents a summary and conclusions.

Savings in Latin America: An Overview

Table 1 presents data on national savings (public plus private) as a fraction of gross domestic product (GDP) in 18 Latin American countries for the period 1986-1993. The (unweighted) averages suggest that national savings rates have risen modestly over the period. Notable success stories include Chile, whose savings rate rose from 10.4 percent of GDP in 1986 to 21.7 percent in 1993, and Honduras, whose savings rate rose from 8 to 18 percent over the same period.

However, national savings rates decline dramatically in three notable cases, namely Argentina, Mexico, and Peru. Like other countries in Latin America, these three countries underwent reform with considerable success during the 1980s and 1990s.[4] After years of failed plans and inaction, policy measures such as deficit reduction, tax reform, trade liberalization, privatization, and deregulation were implemented.

The reforms have brought many good results, including reduced inflation, higher growth, and more efficient allocation of resources. Nonetheless, Figure 1 shows that national (private plus public) savings for these countries have been declining since 1979 but fell sharply in the late 1980s or early 1990s.[5] Tables 2 through 4, which present selected variables

Table 1.
National Savings/GDP, Latin America
1986 - 1993

Country	1986	1987	1988	1989	1990	1991	1992	1993
Argentina	0.148	0.157	0.174	0.138	0.172	0.143	0.138	0.155
Bolivia	0.025	0.026	0.057	0.067	0.074	0.076		
Brazil	0.171	0.217	0.240	0.289	0.221	0.193	0.213	0.202
Chile	0.104	0.155	0.196	0.206	0.225	0.217	0.219	0.217
Colombia	0.188	0.183	0.190	0.176	0.180	0.203	0.178	
Costa Rica	0.150	0.115	0.124	0.113	0.137	0.180	0.152	0.169
Dominican Republic	0.187	0.201	0.279	0.239	0.191	0.164	0.159	0.222
Ecuador	0.136	0.120	0.159	0.155	0.169	0.157	0.196	0.174
El Salvador	0.127	0.122	0.103	0.082	0.079	0.099	0.130	0.145
Guatemala	0.099	0.061	0.081	0.094	0.099	0.102	0.089	0.101
Haiti	0.124	0.138	0.131	0.140	0.128			
Honduras	0.078	0.077	0.120	0.147	0.141	0.120	0.137	0.179
Mexico	0.184	0.215	0.179	0.153	0.156	0.143	0.133	
Panama	0.241	0.234	0.221	0.102	0.104	0.139	0.197	0.245
Paraguay	0.168	0.129	0.197	0.286	0.187	0.185	0.126	
Peru	0.159	0.159	0.187	0.172	0.123	0.112	0.113	0.123
Uruguay	0.106	0.095	0.122	0.132	0.130	0.124	0.130	0.125
Venezuela	0.120	0.146	0.077	0.145	0.234	0.157	0.113	0.104
Average (Unweighted)	0.140	0.142	0.158	0.158	0.153	0.148	0.151	0.166

Source: International Monetary Fund International Financial Statistics (IFS).

Figure 1.
National Savings
Selected Latin American Countries

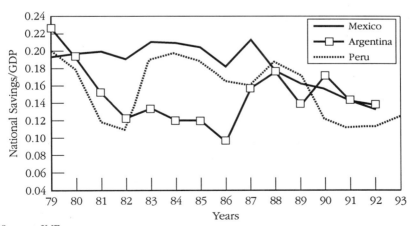

Source: IMF

Table 2.
Selected Variables, Mexico

| | | As a fraction of GDP | | | | | |
| | | Govern-ment Budget | Invest-ment | Private Sector Cons. | Govern-ment Cons. | Curr. Account | Savings | GDP Growth |
Year	Inflation							
1979		-0.0358	0.2342	0.6438	0.1090	-0.0406	0.2295	0.0825
1980	0.2642	-0.0313	0.2413	0.6199	0.1082	-0.0438	0.2288	0.0195
1981	0.2790	0.0671	0.2581	0.6130	0.1172	-0.0582	0.1327	0.0832
1982	0.5895	0.1589	0.2295	0.6315	0.1157	-0.0383	0.0322	0.0795
1983	1.0177	-0.0795	0.1734	0.6041	0.0928	0.0379	0.2907	-0.0061
1984	0.6554	-0.0728	0.1839	0.6076	0.0952	0.0245	0.2812	-0.0417
1985	0.5773	-0.0873	0.1985	0.6714	0.0965	0.0064	0.2921	0.03612
1986	0.8620	-0.1315	0.1948	0.6850	0.0901	-0.0129	0.3134	0.02591
1987	1.3185	-0.1356	0.1844	0.6578	0.0878	0.0283	0.3482	-0.0375
1988	1.1433	-0.1033	0.1926	0.6941	0.0864	-0.0142	0.2817	0.0125
1989	0.2006	-0.0522	0.1817	0.7031	0.0845	-0.0192	0.2147	0.0335
1990	0.2658	0.0074	0.1861	0.7086	0.0845	-0.0292	0.1495	0.0444
1991	0.2270		0.1947	0.7180	0.0901	-0.0519	0.1428	0.0363
1992	0.1548		0.2080	0.7223	0.1008	-0.0753	0.1326	0.0281
1993	0.0974							

Table 3.
Selected Variables, Argentina

| | | As a fraction of GDP | | | | | |
| | | Govern-ment Budget | Invest-ment | Private Sector Cons. | Curr. Account | Savings | GDP growth |
Year	Inflation						
1979		-0.0280	0.2308	0.6573	-0.0047	0.2541	
1980	1.0000	-0.0353	0.2226	0.6360	-0.0304	0.2276	0.0071
1981	1.0400	-0.0818	0.1855	0.6873	-0.0343	0.2330	-0.0636
1982	1.6520	-0.0716	0.1649	0.6811	-0.0413	0.1952	-0.0038
1983	3.4418	-0.1274	0.1726	0.6470	-0.0392	0.2608	-0.0492
1984	5.5000	-0.0506	0.1990	0.7700	-0.0321	0.1900	0.0266
1985	6.6923	-0.0733	0.1344	0.7131	-0.0144	0.1932	-0.0437
1986	0.9000	-0.0269	0.1313	0.7805	-0.0346	0.1236	0.0561
1987	1.3158	-0.0301	0.1965	0.8053	-0.0383	0.1883	0.0254
1988	3.4828	-0.0189	0.1892	0.7838	-0.0125	0.1956	-0.0188
1989	30.8692	-0.0038	0.1551	0.7802	-0.0170	0.1418	-0.0622
1990	23.1371	-0.0140	0.1400	0.8027	0.0322	0.1722	0.0006
1991	1.7200	-0.0040	0.1464	0.8377	-0.0037	0.1427	0.0890
1992	0.2463	0.0030	0.1670	0.8483	-0.0294	0.1376	0.0865
1993	0.1062						

Table 4.
Selected Variables, Peru

		As a fraction of GDP						
Year	Inflation	Govern-ment Budget	Invest-ment	Private Sector Cons.	Govern-ment Cons.	Curr. Account	Savings	GDP Growth
1979		0.0058	0.1414	0.6355	0.0965	0.0596	0.1952	
1980	0.5924	0.0286	0.1729	0.6680	0.1282	0.0037	0.1479	0.0290
1981	0.7500	-0.0489	0.2040	0.6961	0.1289	-0.0860	0.1669	0.0304
1982	0.6457	-0.0398	0.2202	0.6831	0.1385	-0.1115	0.1485	0.0089
1983	1.1146	-0.0764	0.2357	0.6465	0.1115	-0.0446	0.2675	-0.1198
1984	1.1111	-0.0478	0.2087	0.6580	0.0971	-0.0118	0.2447	0.0510
1985	1.6316	-0.0213	0.1809	0.6543	0.0957	0.0079	0.2100	0.0278
1986	0.7800	-0.0361	0.2056	0.7028	0.0972	-0.0419	0.1998	0.0924
1987	0.8596	-0.0623	0.1981	0.6981	0.0997	-0.0386	0.2218	-0.0821
1988	6.6616	-0.0360	0.2246	0.7111	0.0743	-0.0373	0.2232	-0.1103
1989	33.7105	-0.0562	0.1698	0.7358	0.0660	0.0024	0.2284	-0.0425
1990	74.8150	-0.0365	0.1471	0.7749	0.0627	-0.0246	0.1590	0.0284
1991	4.1000	-0.0143	0.1434	0.7979	0.0549	-0.0313	0.1264	-0.0235
1992	0.7333	-0.0177	0.1534	0.7976	0.0664	-0.0407	0.1304	0.0644
1993	0.4864		0.1672	0.7813	0.0652	-0.0438	0.1233	

from these countries for these years,[6] show some similarities across countries. In all three countries, inflation grew throughout the 1980s and then fell. The most successful disinflation occurred in Argentina, where hyperinflation iin 1989-1990 had become a yearly inflation rate of 3 percent by 1994. Peru had the least success at taming inflation. Although Peru ended its hyperinflation, yearly inflation in 1993 was 48 percent. All countries in the group reduced their public sector deficits, in some years obtaining surpluses.[7]

Inflation peaked in Mexico and Argentina in 1989 and in Peru in 1990. Thereafter, private sector consumption and gross capital formation increased as fractions of GDP in all three countries. At the same time, government budget deficits and current account surpluses, as a fraction of GDP, fell.

The above discussion suggests three possible explanations for the decline in savings. First, savings may be responding to a rise in expected future income. That is, agents respond to the expectation of increased GDP growth in the future by consuming more now. Second, an increase in public savings (a cut in the deficit) might be offset by a decrease in private sector savings. Finally, more stable economic environments, with lower inflation rates, might have encouraged more borrowing and greater spending.

Do Savings Fall in Anticipation of Higher Future Income?

Reforms in Latin America, including regulatory and tax reform, may signal a rise in future income. Thus, according to the permanent income hypothesis (PIH), savings should fall and consumption should rise today. Unfortunately, the PIH is difficult to verify, mainly because permanent income is not directly observable. There are accepted established methods to test the PIH. The traditional method, following Friedman (1956), for example, is to construct a time-series estimate of permanent income. Unfortunately, GDP and consumption data for most Latin American countries may not be of sufficient quality to merit such techniques. Rather, GDP and consumption data are recorded on a yearly basis for most countries. It would be difficult to separate the recent temporary and permanent components of GDP with this data.[8]

An alternative method would be to test for forward-looking behavior. Campbell (1987) and Campbell and Deaton (1989) suggest that if people "save for a rainy day," lagged savings should be negatively correlated with current period income. As shown in the papers mentioned above, a two-equation vector autoregression (VAR) containing the savings ratio (S/Y) and the growth of output (%ΔY) has two implications for the PIH. First, the PIH, combined with rational expectations, implies specific restrictions on the coefficients of the above-mentioned VAR (see Campbell and Deaton 1989). Second, even if these restrictions are rejected, consumers may exhibit forward-looking behavior. Evidence that the lagged savings ratio S/Y causes (in the Granger sense) GDP growth %ΔY with a negative coefficient indicates behavior and consumption smoothing, key elements of the PIH. More precisely, Campbell (1987) and Campbell and Deaton (1989) note that a test of the PIH can be expressed in the form of a vector autoregression (VAR) such as

$$(1) \qquad \mathbf{X}_t = \mathbf{a}_0 + \mathbf{a}_1 \mathbf{X}_{t-1} + \mathbf{a}_2 \mathbf{X}_{t-2} + \mathbf{a}_3 \mathbf{X}_{t-3} + \ldots + \mathbf{a}_k \mathbf{X}_{t-k} + \mathbf{e}_t$$

where $\mathbf{X}_t$ is the vector of variables $[S/Y_t, \%\Delta Y_t]$, $\mathbf{a}_i$ is the corresponding vector of reduced form coefficients, and $\mathbf{e}_t$ is a vector of error terms. Campbell (1987) and Campbell and Deaton (1989) develop cross-equation restrictions for a system similar to system (1). Essentially, these restrictions imply that consumption follows a random walk, such as that discussed by Robert Hall (1978).[9] Although these restrictions were rejected in previous studies, VAR system (1) is still useful, as it can also be used to test for evidence of forward-looking behavior. Specifically, if consumers "save for a rainy day," increases in savings should precede (Granger-cause) reductions in income.

Thus, the test of forward-looking behavior to be performed is the second equation from system (1):

$$(1') \qquad \%\Delta Y_{jt} = \sum_{j=1}^{J} \theta_j D_j + \sum_{i=1}^{I} \alpha_{yi} \%\Delta Y_{j,t-i} + \sum_{i=1}^{I} \alpha_{si} S/Y_{j,\,t-i} + error_{j,t}$$

where J is the number of countries (18), D is a country-specific dummy, and I is the number of lags (2).[10] The equation is estimated using panel data. (For further discussion of panel-data VARs, see Holtz-Eakin, Newey, and Rosen 1988 and 1989.)[11] In this regression, the null hypothesis to be tested is that the a_{si} sum to zero. For the case of the sum of the a_{si} statistically different from zero and negative, there is evidence favoring the "rainy day" hypothesis.

Prior to estimation, two preliminary issues must be addressed. First, the most correct measure of private savings should include the inflation adjustment on government debt. That is, private savings is defined as the current account surplus, plus investment, minus the government's deficit. As discussed in the data appendix, the inflation-adjusted government deficit equals expenditures on goods, services, and interest payments, minus taxes and the inflation adjustment. However, it is not possible to obtain an exact measure of the inflation adjustment. Instead, because most government debt in the countries in question is held within the banking system, public sector credit within the banking system may be used as an approximation. Thus, the regressions will be run with both the non-inflation-adjusted measures as well as the inflation-adjusted measures.

Second, in order for inferences from equation (1') to be valid, the variables in question must be stationary. Thus, the stationarity test developed by Kwaitkowski et al. (1992) is presented in an appendix. Results confirm the stationarity of both $\%\Delta Y$ and S/Y, in most cases.[12]

Results from regression equation (1) are presented in Table 5. Critically, the sum of the α_{si} is negative, suggesting forward-looking behavior. Furthermore, an exclusion test (that is, a test that the sum of the α_{si} equals zero) indicates rejection of the null hypothesis at greater than the 99 percent level for the non-inflation-adjusted measure and 90 percent for the inflation-adjusted measure. The evidence, therefore, favors forward-looking behavior in determining savings.

Are Private and Public Savings Substitutes?

It is also possible that private savings move in the opposite direction of public savings. Recent approaches to fiscal policy have stressed the consolidation of private and public sector budget constraints.[13] This fact has given rise to several related propositions. One implication is that public and private sector savings are perfect substitutes. If consumption decisions incorporate current and future policy and government spending remains constant in all periods, a one-dollar increase in the government's budget deficit should be offset by a one-dollar increase in private sector savings. An alternative way of stating this proposition is that tax and bond finance may be equivalent. This is the Ricardian Equivalence Proposition (REP), whose current popularity is due largely to an article by Barro (1974). According to this hypothesis, for a given value of government expenditures (in present discounted value terms), bond finance and tax finance are equivalent.[14]

Table 5.
Test for Forward-Looking Behavior in Savings,
Equation (1')

Coefficient Estimates	Inflation Adjustment Not Included	Inflation Adjustment Included
α_{y1}	0.283	0.292
	(0.045)	(0.045)
α_{y2}	0.054	0.053
	(0.044)	(0.045)
α_{s1}	-0.040	0.047
	(0.047)	(0.043)
α_{s2}	-0.118	-0.104
	(0.047)	(0.042)
R^2 Adjusted	0.157	0.140
F-statistic, exclusion of $\Sigma\alpha_{si}$	8.278	3.170

In a study of 13 developing countries, Corbo and Schmidt-Hebbel (1991) find evidence suggesting that a one-dollar increase in public savings causes an approximate 50-cent decrease in private savings. For Latin America, some casual empiricism also suggests public savings crowds out private savings. For example, in Tables 1 through 3, the reductions in government budget deficits in Mexico, Argentina, and Peru clearly accompany the downswing in private savings. Moreover, panel data on private savings [S(private)] and the public savings [S(public)], as shown in Figure 2, also display a negative relationship.

The substitution of private and public savings will be examined econometrically. The basic regression equation is

$$(2) \quad S(private)/Y_{jt} = \sum_{j=1}^{J}\theta_j D_j + a_1 S(public)/Y + \mathbf{X}_t \mathbf{b} + error_{j,t}$$

where D_j is a dummy variable equal to 1 for country j but 0 otherwise. The vector $\mathbf{X}_t$ contains other relevant variables.[15] Variables that should be in $\mathbf{X}$ include GDP growth (%Δ Y) and world interest rates (%Δr*). This latter variable reflects the view of Calvo, Leiderman, and Reinhardt (1993) that shocks from the world economy have been important determinants of consumption and savings in Latin America. Finally, another variable that should appear in the vector $\mathbf{X}$ is inflation, which is a tax on financial

Figure 2.
Private and Public Savings in Latin America

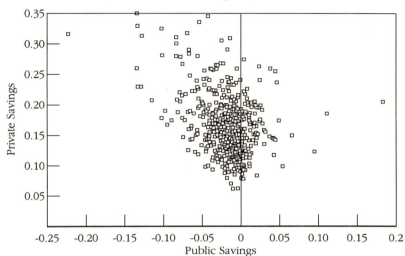

intermediation. Also, uncertainty regarding inflation introduces "noise" into a financial system, increasing the cost for banks and other financial intermediaries to do their work to bring lending and borrowing units together. A reduction in inflation, therefore, facilitates borrowing and consumption.[16]

Equation (2) alternatively may be thought of as a test of the effects of a government budget deficit jointly on the current account (CA/Y) and investment (I/Y), since

(3) $\partial S(private)/\partial S(public) = \partial CA/\partial S(public) + \partial I/\partial S(public) - 1$

Thus, to examine the two related issues of the effect of public savings on the current account and investment, the following regressions are also run:

(4) $CA/Y_{jt} = \sum_{j=1}^{J} \theta_j D_j + a_{1c} S(public)/Y + \mathbf{X}_t \mathbf{b} + error_{j,t}$

(5) $I/Y_{jt} = \sum_{j=1}^{J} \theta_j D_j + a_{11} S(public)/Y + \mathbf{X}_t \mathbf{b} + error_{j,t}$

Econometric preliminaries are similar for those previous estimates. First, the stationarity of variables must be considered. Results in Table 6 suggest that, with few exceptions, the relevant variables are stationary. Second, there is the issue of simultaneous equations bias. S(public) may be correlated with the error term. A simple remedy, replacement of contemporaneous values with lagged values of S(public), is applied.

The results suggest a high degree of offset between public and private savings. Considering the contemporaneous model, a one-point increase in non-inflation-adjusted S(public)/Y reduces private sector savings by .85, while a one-point increase in the inflation-adjusted measure reduces private sector savings by 0.9. In both cases, the null hypotheses that the coefficients $\partial[S(private)/Y]/\partial[S(public)/Y] = 0$ are rejected at the 99 percent level or greater. Using the lagged values, the offset is somewhat less. For the non-inflation-adjusted measure, $\partial[S(private)/Y]/\partial[S(public)/Y]$ is estimated to be -0.71, while for the inflation-adjusted measure, this estimate is approximately 0.55.

The large impacts of public savings on private savings are reflected in a smaller but statistically significant impact on the current account and little impact on investment. Regarding the current account, a contemporaneous change in public sector savings yields estimates ranging from 0.09 (inflation-adjusted) to 0.26 (non-inflation-adjusted). For the lagged measure, estimates range from 0.02 (inflation-adjusted) to 0.11 (non-inflation-adjusted). All estimates except the lagged, inflation-adjusted measures are significantly different from zero at the 95 percent level or greater.

Regarding the relationship between investment and public sector savings, only one of the four estimates yielded a significant relationship. The contemporaneous estimate without the inflation adjustment is -0.12. In all other cases, the estimates of this coefficient are not significantly different from zero.

The results of this section may be summarized as follows. Public and private savings appear to be strongly negatively related. Estimates of $\partial[S(private)/Y]/\partial[S(public)/Y]$ range from -0.56 to -0.90 and are significantly different from zero in all cases. Public savings have some impact on the current account. Estimates of $\partial[CA/Y]/\partial[S(public)/Y]$ range from -0.56 to -0.90 and are statistically different from zero in all cases. Finally, public savings appear to have little impact on investment; in three of four cases, estimates of $\partial[I/Y]/\partial[S(public)/Y]$ are not significantly different from zero.

Fiscal Policy and Private Consumption

An alternative way to address the relationship between private and public savings is to examine directly the effect of fiscal variables on consumption.[17] Recent literature has examined the link between private consumption and fiscal policy in several ways. The approach taken here will be to develop a reduced form consumption equation, similar to Feldstein (1982), Kormendi (1983), Modigliani and Sterling (1986), Barth, Iden, and Russek (1986), and others.[18]

Table 6.
Effects of Public Savings on Private Savings, Current Account, and Investment Pooled Data, Latin America Coefficient Estimates
(Standard Errors in Parentheses)

Equation (2), (4), (5) Contemporaneous Explanatory Variables

Dependent Variable	S(priv)/Y	CA/Y	I/Y	S(priv)/Y	CA/Y	I/Y
Explanatory Variable	**Without Inflation Adjustment**			**With Inflation Adjustment**		
S(public)/Y	-0.8599	0.2686	-0.1287	-0.9003	-0.0913	-0.0083
	(0.0555)	(0.0480)	(0.0524)	(0.0412)	(0.0366)	(0.0393)
%ΔY	0.1427	-0.0871	0.2299	0.1713	-0.0444	0.2159
	(0.0426)	(0.0368)	(0.0402)	(0.0419)	(0.0372)	(0.0400)
π	0.0003	0.0008	-0.0005	-0.0000	0.0002	-0.0002
	(0.0004)	(0.0003)	(0.0003)	(0.0003)	(0.0003)	(0.0003)
Δr*	0.0004	-0.0002	0.0007	0.0005	-0.0000	0.0005
	(0.0008)	(0.0007)	(0.0008)	(0.0008)	(0.0007)	(0.0008)
R^2 adjusted	0.5480	0.2852	0.3917	0.6854	0.2493	0.3794

Equation (2), (4), (5) Contemporaneous Explanatory Variables

Dependent Variable	S(priv)/Y	CA/Y	I/Y	S(priv)/Y	CA/Y	I/Y
Explanatory Variable	**Without Inflation Adjustment**			**With Inflation Adjustment**		
S(public)/Y	-0.7157	0.1119	-0.0228	-0.5561	0.0202	0.0446
	0.0656	0.0490	0.0518	0.0546	0.0365	0.0387
%ΔY	0.1709	-0.0645	0.2185	0.1674	-0.0450	0.2109
	0.0496	0.0374	0.0397	0.0540	0.0372	0.0394
π	-0.0031	0.0000	-0.0004	-0.0031	-0.0003	-0.0002
	0.0004	0.0003	0.0003	0.0005	0.0003	0.0003
Δr*	-0.0008	-0.0023	0.0014	-0.0009	-0.0022	0.0015
	0.0010	0.0007	0.0008	0.0011	0.0007	0.0008
R^2 Adjusted	0.4106	0.2645	0.4033	0.4933	0.2586	0.4012

Notes: %DY = percent change real GDP, p = inflation, Dr* = change in U.S. Federal Funds Rate.

The basic equation is

$$(6) \qquad C/Y_{jt} = \sum_{j=1}^{J} \theta_j D_j + a_G\, G/Y_{it} + a_T\, T/Y_{it} + \mathbf{X}_t \mathbf{b} + error_{j,t}$$

where G/Y and T/Y are the ratios of government expenditures and tax revenues, respectively, to GDP. This regression captures the separate effects of G and T on consumption. Consider first the effect of G. Government expenditures should impact negatively on consumption for two reasons. First, government purchase substitutes for private consumption. Second, higher government expenditures imply a higher tax burden. The effect of taxes (T) is ambiguous. Holding other fiscal variables constant and if the Ricardian Equivalence Hypothesis (REH) holds, taxes should have no effect on consumption. However, a negative effect of taxes on consumption may indicate the presence of liquidity-constrained consumers.[19]

Equation (6) may be modified to estimate the effect of public savings [S(public)] on consumption. If the non-inflation-adjusted measure is used, the coefficients of G and T are constrained to be of equal but opposite magnitude. However, if S(public) is inflation adjusted, its effect on consumption may differ from that of G/Y - T/Y. The effect of public savings on consumption is ambiguous. According to the REH, deficits per se should have no effect on consumption, although S(public) may affect consumption for other reasons. First, an increase in public savings may capture increases in taxes or decreases in government expenditures. Second, as Aschauer (1985) points out, deficits may impact negatively on consumption because they signal higher taxes in the future. Thus, the effect of an increase in public sector savings on consumption is uncertain. Two regressions are estimated. Following Corbo and Schmidt-Hebbel (1991), one equation is

$$(7) \qquad C/Y_{jt} = \sum_{j=1}^{J} \theta_j D_j + a_s\, S(public)/Y + \mathbf{X}_t \mathbf{b} + error_{j,t}$$

Also, if the inflation-adjusted measure of S(public) is used, the following regression may be estimated:

$$(8) \qquad C/Y_{jt} = \sum_{j=1}^{J} \theta_j D_j + a_G\, G/Y + a_T\, T/Y + a_s\, S(public)/Y + \mathbf{X}_t \mathbf{b} + error_{j,t}$$

Equation (8) permits separate estimation of the substitution of government expenditures for private consumption, tax revenue effects, and wealth effects due to changes in public savings. To address the issue of exogeniety, equations (6), (7), and (8) are estimated with both contemporaneous and lagged variables. The contemporaneous version is reported in Table 7, and the lagged version is reported in Table 8. According to both versions, there is a strong, negative relationship between consumption and government expenditures.

According to equation (6), a one-point increase in G/Y results in a 0.26-point decrease in C/Y. If the inflation-adjusted budget deficit is added to equation (8), the coefficient rises in absolute terms to -0.37. Both coefficients are significant at the 95 percent level or higher. The results also apply to the lagged version of equation (6) in Table 8. Here, the reduction of consumption from a one-point increase in G/Y is between -0.35 (column 1) and -0.45 (column 4). In both cases, the coefficients are significant at the 95 percent confidence level or higher.

There is little evidence that taxes affect consumption. In only one version, the lagged version excluding the inflation-adjusted deficit (Table 8, equation (8)) is the estimate of the coefficient of T/Y on consumption significantly different from zero. In this case, the estimated coefficient -0.17 is significant at the 95 percent level. In all other estimates, the effect of T/Y on C/Y is not significantly different from zero.

Table 7.
Consumption Equation (6)-(8) Contemporaneous
Explanatory Variables Coefficient Estimates
(Standard Errors in Parentheses)

Explanatory Variables	Equation (6)	Equation (7)	Equation (7)	Equation (8)
	Dependent Variable: Private Consumption/GDP			
G/Y	-0.2672			-0.3741
	(0.0660)			(0.0906)
T/Y	-0.1709			-0.0046
	(0.0750)			(0.1097)
S(public)/Y [a]		-0.1334		
		(0.0674)		
S(public)/Y [b]			0.0725	0.1577
			(0.0497)	(0.0718)
%Δy	-0.1187	-0.0632	-0.0720	-0.1405
	(0.0492)	(0.0517)	(0.0506)	(0.0497)
π	-0.0003	-0.0006	-0.0009	-0.0001
	(0.0004)	(0.0004)	(0.0004)	(0.0004)
Δr*	-0.0019	-0.0016	-0.0012	-0.0018
	(0.0009)	(0.0010)	(0.0009)	(0.0009)
R^2 adjusted	0.8011	0.7780	0.7796	0.8027

[a] measure of S(public) excludes inflation adjustment.
[b] measure of S(public) includes inflation adjustment.

Table 8.
Consumption Equations (6)-(8) Lagged Explanatory
Variables Coefficient Estimates
(Standard Errors in Parentheses)

Explanatory Variables	Dependent Variable: Private Consumption/GDP			
	Equation (6)	Equation (7)	Equation (7)	Equation (8)
G/Y	-0.3532			-0.4552
	(0.0660)			(0.0912)
T/Y	-0.0556			0.08266
	(0.0755)			(0.1109)
S(public)/Y [a]		0.2337		
		(0.0671)		
S(public)/Y [b]			-0.0080	-0.1233
			(0.0503)	(0.0723)
%Δy	-0.1368	-0.0835	-0.0712	-0.1554
	(0.0493)	(0.0513)	(0.0513)	(0.0501)
π	0.0008	0.0004	-0.0001	0.0008
	(0.0004)	(0.0004)	(0.0004)	(0.0004)
Δr*	-0.0012	-0.0009	-0.0006	-0.0013
	(0.0009)	(0.0010)	(0.0010)	(0.0010)
R^2 adjusted	0.8033	0.7849	0.7782	0.8035

[a] measure of S(public) excludes inflation adjustment.
[b] measure of S(public) includes inflation adjustment.

To summarize, the results of this section present evidence favoring a consolidated budget constraint (a Ricardian view). In all cases, increases in government expenditures reduced consumption. At the same time, the effects of tax revenues are, for the most part, statistically insignificant. Finally, the effect of public savings on consumption was ambiguous and dependent on the measure used.

Policy Response to Reductions in Savings

Evidently, policymakers are aware that savings may fall during stabilizations. In several countries in Latin America, where stabilization packages have included measures to discourage increases in private consumption levels, such policies have had unintended side effects and have encouraged policymakers to delay reform in critical areas.

Credit controls are one such policy. As part of Brazil's Plano Real of 1994, the government imposed credit controls and taxed consumption borrowing. There were difficulties with this policy, however, as lenders and borrowers found ways to circumvent it.[20] Moreover, the underlying problem, reform of the domestic financial system, was delayed.

Another way to discourage consumption is to maintain high real interest rates.[21] Unfortunately, such a policy has unintended side effects, such as to attract foreign capital, which further increase the domestic money supply. The policy of high interest rates, which drew "hot capital" to Mexico, may have played a role in the peso's collapse in December 1994.

Conclusions

Much recent evidence, especially from Asian economies, suggests that savings encourage growth. Hence, higher domestic savings are, in general, desirable. Chile is a notable example of a Latin American country that increased savings and has grown at rates higher than the Latin American average.

Simultaneously, increasing savings rates may be difficult, especially during macroeconomic stabilization. As a result of optimizing behavior, private savings may fall when more stable macroeconomic policies bring higher public sector savings, lower inflation, and anticipated increases in future output. For example, according to the results of this study, the offset of public savings by private savings is sizable, between 0.7 and 0.9 basis points as a percent of GDP. This is somewhat larger than some previous estimates. For example, Corbo and Schmidt-Hebbel (1991) estimate this offset to be around 0.5.

Nonetheless, cuts to government budget deficits should raise national savings. The analysis above suggests that, while deficit cutting is offset by reductions in private sector savings, a reduction in the deficit will, on net, yield an increase in national savings.

An important question not addressed in this paper is how national and foreign savings substitute for one another. Several authors (see, for example, Calvo, Leiderman, and Reinhardt 1993) suggest that most of the shocks to the real exchange rate and capital flows emanate from the world economy rather than domestically. They recommend some sort of restrictions on capital movements, for example, a tax on short-term capital flows. The recent crisis in Mexico and its extension to other Latin American countries suggest that one damaging aspect of greater foreign capital flows is their ability to leave so quickly, forcing domestic banks to liquidate loans. A remedy for this might be higher reserve requirements on foreign capital flows, which are equivalent to a tax on such flows.

What effect should such measures directed at foreign capital inflows have on private (and hence national) savings? Clearly, such policies increase the cost of borrowing from abroad, but would they encourage additional savings? It is instructive to note that Chile, which experienced high growth and savings, has imposed a mild system of capital controls since the early 1980s. These controls, however, are being eliminated at this time.

Data Appendix

All data taken from the International Monetary Fund's International Financial Statistics.

G = government expenditures, domestic currency, Series 82

T = tax revenue, domestic currency, Series 81

π = percentage change in GDP deflator Series 99b/Series 99.b

Y = nominal GDP, Series 99b

y = real income, Series 99b.p

C = personal consumption, Series 96

S(public), not inflation adjusted = T - g

S(public) inflation adjusted = S(public) not inflation adjusted + π (Series 51)

CA = Current account S 77a.d

I = investment Series 93.e

S(private), not inflation adjusted = CA + I - S(public) not inflation adjusted

S(private), inflation adjusted = CA + I - S(public) inflation adjusted

National Savings = S(private) + S(public)

Appendix. Stationarity Tests
Null Hypothesis of Stationarity Test due
to Kwaitkowski et al. (1992)

	Variable S(private)/Y		S(public)/Y		I/Y		CA/Y		%DY	
	2-lag	4-lag	2-lag	4-lag	2-lag	4-lag	2-lag	4-lag	2-lag	4-lag
Argentina	0.204	0.167	0.229	0.292	0.126	0.149	0.210	0.258	0.534*	0.433**
Bolivia	0.098	0.123	0.127	0.139	0.217	0.194	0.286	0.251	0.340**	0.269
Brazil	0.181	0.149	0.275	0.213	0.244	0.246	0.307	0.285	0.490**	0.411**
Chile	0.145	0.129	0.075	0.094	0.248	0.325**	0.257	0.201	0.064	0.080
Colombia	0.203	0.223	0.095	0.102	0.166	0.151	0.088	0.093	0.139	0.188
Costa Rica	0.082	0.124	0.104	0.130	0.099	0.102	0.131	0.129	0.291	0.293
Dom. Rep.	0.519**	0.474	0.195	0.178	0.165	0.196	0.259	0.255	0.199	0.159
Ecuador	0.136	0.143	0.146	0.209	0.080	0.093	0.058	0.078	0.388*	0.375*
El Salvador	0.168	0.148	0.091	0.091	0.145	0.120	0.077	0.095	0.085	0.106
Guatemala	0.283	0.215	0.105	0.112	0.134	0.115	0.453**	0.368	0.283	0.245
Haiti	0.203	0.247	0.152	0.156	0.146	0.145	0.223	0.177	0.335*	0.303
Honduras	0.139	0.212	0.093	0.096	0.198	0.200	0.135	0.154	0.145	0.184
Mexico	0.223	0.243	0.339*	0.376*	0.088	0.110	0.187	0.207	0.300	0.288
Panama	0.157	0.171	0.216	0.162	0.555**	0.496**	0.395**	0.400	0.301	0.302
Paraguay	0.173	0.167	0.190	0.235	0.096	0.096	0.237	0.244	0.129	0.124
Peru	0.186	0.171	0.130	0.172	0.158	0.202	0.057	0.093	0.093	0.144
Uruguay	0.051	0.116	0.054	0.070	0.097	0.096	0.140	0.156	0.067	0.103
Venezuela	0.302	0.233	0.120	0.163	0.193	0.201	0.063	0.109	0.118	0.113

Critical values for rejection of null-hypothesis of stationarity: .34 (90%), .44 (95%).

Rejections of the null hypothesis of stationarity for the 90% and 95% levels are denoted by single asterisk (*) and double asterisk (**), respectively.

Notes

1. This is especially true in light of the recent evidence linking savings and growth, such as by Mankiw, Roemer, and Weil 1992.

2. Perfect substitution of private and public sector is often referred to as Ricardian Equivalence.

3. This idea follows the work of Bernanke (1983).

4. The periods of major reform successes are 1987-1989 for Mexico, 1989-1991 for Argentina, and 1990-1991 for Peru.

5. Private savings measures are difficult to obtain. In this paper, savings are computed from the national income identity:

S(private) = Current Account + Investment - Government Budget Surplus.

Thus, national savings is simply the sum of S(private) and the Government Budget Surplus. To incorporate inflation's effects on government obligations, two different definitions of the government budget surplus are used.

6. Data are not yet available for Brazil's Real Plan of 1994. Nonetheless, early evidence suggests a fall in savings.

7. Surpluses were obtained by adjustment of expenditures and revenues, not by "inflating away" the debt or otherwise defaulting. An exception is Argentina's BONEX plan of 1990.

8. In order to do this, one would have to obtain estimates of permanent income and a consumption function with stable and precise parameters. This task is very difficult for the industrialized countries, who enjoy much more accurate consumption data, generally available on a quarterly basis.

9. This can be seen by considering a simple example. Note that

$$-(c_t - c_{c-1}) \approx (y_t - c_t) - (y_t - y_{t-1}) - (y_{t-1} - c_{t-1})$$

where c= consumption and $S_t = (y_t - c_t)$. In the case of a 1-lag VAR, $(y_t - c_t) = a_{10} + a_{11} (y_{t-1} - c_{t-1}) + a_{12} (y_t - y_{t-1}) + e_{1t}$ and $(y_t - y_{t-1}) = a_{20} + a_{21} (y_{t-1} - c_{t-1}) + a_{22} (y_t - y_{t-1}) + e_{2t}$. An implication of the PIH, as discussed in Hall (1978), is that no past information helps explain $c_t - c_{t-1}$. Thus, the corresponding restrictions are $(a_{11} - a_{21} - 1) = 0$ and $(a_{12} - a_{22}) = 0$. Note also that the above may be easily cast in terms of ratios of consumption and savings to GDP and GDP growth.

10. Also, 3 and 4 lags were tried. The results, not reported, yield similar conclusions to the 2-lag case.

11. While the VAR technique is most often used for time-series data, Holtz-Eakin, Newey, and Rosen (1988) note that VARs may be easily used with pooled data. In general, pooling is desirable when there are many panel units (countries)

but few time-series observations. While the system may be estimated with non-stationary variables, HNR note that, if the variables are stationary, the procedure is simplified. Another consideration is whether the coefficient parameters are constant over time. HNR discuss an instrumental variables procedure to uncover time-varying components. However, they note that such a procedure is unnecessary for Granger causality tests like those presented below. Thus, estimates are ordinary least squares. Also, estimates include country-specific intercepts. HNR note that, since intercepts may differ across panel units, such a procedure is correct in the current econometric context.

12. A key difference between this test and others (such as the Augmented Dickey Fuller, Za, and Zt tests) is that the null hypothesis is one of stationarity, rather than non-stationarity. Variables expressed as ratios of GDP, as well as GDP growth, should be bounded, and hence stationary. For this reason, the null of stationarity is appropriate.

13. This point was originally made by Bailey (1971). A commonly cited exposition of this point of view is found in Barro's (1993) macroeconomics textbook. See also Kormendi (1983).

14. Barro's revival of the REH was originally met with skepticism. A series of articles (including Feldstein 1982, Kormendi 1983, Aschauer 1985) attempted to test the REH and related propositions using U.S. data. These articles presented evidence more favorable to the REH than might have been predicted by earlier Keynesian viewpoints. As a result, the REH could no longer be easily dismissed. Indeed, one recent review of the literature (Seater 1993) goes somewhat further by suggesting that the evidence in favor of the REH is much stronger than that against.

15. The inclusion of country dummies implies a fixed, country-specific effect. Variable country effects may be modeled as well, with a generalized least squares procedure.

16. Casual observation suggests that, as a whole, financial services have grown as economies stabilized. For example, in Mexico, credit to the private sector rose from 11 percent of GDP in 1984 to 33 percent in 1992. At least two authors have used Mexican data to test the effect of increased credit on economic activity. Moore (1994) presents evidence that credit, in addition to other variables, Granger-causes GDP in a VAR system. Copelman (1994) estimates a random-walk consumption function (following Hall 1978) that includes credit. According to the assumptions of her model, credit should not explain consumption unless consumers are liquidity constrained. In fact, she rejects the hypothesis that consumers in Mexico are not liquidity constrained. Rather, her evidence suggests that increases in the quantity of loans have a positive impact on consumption.

17. Recall that consumption equals output minus savings minus tax revenue.

18. Of course, a more rigorous approach would be to develop a regression equation based on the Euler equations in an intertemporal optimization framework, similar to Aschauer (1985). Such a model would be a fruitful topic for future research. See also Corbo and Schmidt-Hebbel (1991).

19. That is, some portion of the consuming population may be liquidity constrained. In this case, taxes and consumption should be negatively related. For additional evidence on this topic, see Corbo and Schmidt-Hebbel (1991).

20. For example, the use of pre-dated checks, a common substitute for consumer credit, increased dramatically under the credit controls.

21. The Mexican, Brazilian, and, to a lesser degree, Argentine governments raised interest rates through open market operations.

References

Aschauer, D.A. 1985. "Fiscal Policy and Aggregate Demand." *American Economic Review* 75(1):117-127.

Bailey, M. 1971. *National Income and the Price Level,* 2nd ed. New York: McGraw Hill.

Barro, R. 1974. "Are Government Bonds Net Wealth?" *Journal of Political Economy* 82(6):1095-1117.

Barro, R. 1993. *Macroeconomics.* New York: John Wiley and Sons.

Barth, J., J. Iden, and F. Russek. 1986. "Government Debt, Government Spending, and Private Sector Behavior: Comment." *American Economic Review* 76(5):1158-1167.

Bernanke, B. 1983. "Non-Monetary Effects of the Financial Crisis in the Propagation of the Great Depression." *American Economic Review* 73:257-276.

Campbell, J.Y. 1987. "Does Saving Anticipate Labor Income? An Alternative Test of the Permanent Income Hypothesis." *Econometrica* 55:1249-1273.

Campbell, J.Y., and A. Deaton. 1989. "Why is Consumption So Smooth?" *Review of Economic Studies* 56:357-374.

Calvo, G., L. Leiderman, and C. Reinhardt. 1993. "Internal and External Shocks, Current Accounts, and Real Exchange Rates in Developing Economies." Staff Papers, International Monetary Fund.

Copelman, M. 1994. "The Role of Credit in Post-Stabilization Consumption Booms." Mimeo, Massachusetts Institute of Technology. Department of Economics.

Corbo, V., and K. Schimidt-Hebbel. 1991. "Public Policy and Saving in Developing Economies." *Journal of Development Economics* 36:89-115.

Feldstein, M. 1982. "Government Deficits and Aggregate Demand." *Journal of Monetary Economics* 9(1):1-20.

Friedman, M. 1956. *A Theory of the Consumption Function.* Princeton, N.J.: Princeton University Press.

Hall, Robert. 1978. "Stochastic Implications of the Life-Cycle/Permanent Income Hypothesis: Theory and Evidence." *Journal of Political Economy* 86(6):971-987.

Holtz-Eakin, D., W. Newey, and H.S. Rosen. 1988. "Estimating Vector Autoregressions with Panel Data." *Econometrica* 56:1371-1395.

Holtz-Eakin, D., W. Newey, and H.S. Rosen. 1989. "The Revenues-Expenditures Nexus: Evidence from Local Government Data." *International Economic Review* 30(2):415-429.

Kormendi, R. 1983. "Government Debt, Government Spending, and Private Sector Behavior." *American Economic Review* 73(5): 994-1010.

Kwaitkowski, Denis, Peter C.B. Phillips, Peter Schmidt, and Yongcheol Shin. 1992. "Testing the Null Hypothesis of Stationarity Against the Alternative of a Unit Root." *Journal of Econometrics* 54:159-178.

Mankiw, N.G., David Roemer, and David Weil. 1992. "A Contribution to the Empirics of Economic Growth." *Quarterly Journal of Economics* 107 (May):407-437.

Modigliani, F., and A. Sterling. 1986. "Government Debt, Government Spending, and Private Sector Behavior: Comment." *American Economic Review* 76:1168-1179.

Moore, R. 1994. "The Role of Credit in the Mexican Economy." Mimeo, Federal Reserve Bank of Dallas; Presented at Latin American Econometrics Society Meetings, Caracas, August.

Seater, J. 1993. "Ricardian Equivalence: A Literature Review." *Journal of Economic Literature* 31(1): 142-190.

Chapter 3

Foreign Sources of Long-term Financing for Borrowers in Brazil

Clarice Pechman

Introduction

A nalysis of the sources of Brazil's long-term financing leads to discussion of the country's development process, to which private Brazilian companies, the government, and the foreign sector have all contributed. Basically, two options are available to companies needing to raise outside funds: going into debt or going public. Such funds are derived from savings in the economy, either domestic — private or state — or foreign.

In Brazil, the industrialization process essentially took off, beginning in the 1950s, with the Goals Plan laid down by the Juscelino Kubitschek government. The sustenance of this plan was threefold: state-owned enterprises, Brazilian private capital, and foreign capital.

The scarcity of private savings to finance investment, mainly in basic infrastructure, combined with the incipient structure of domestic financing, led the federal government to create the Brazilian Development Bank (BNDES) in 1952. This development bank was tremendously important to Brazil's industrialization process.

The system of financial institutions fostering development was complemented with the rise of local development banks in the states of the Brazilian federation. The states retained control over the capital stock of these development banks, which were organized as corporations (S/A) with head offices in the state capitals.

The paramount objective of these institutions was to provide the funds required for medium- and long-term financing of programs and projects aimed at fostering economic and social development of their respective states. The priority focus of their support was the private sector.

Among the funding options available, the development banks could draw on third-party funds derived from the following: 1) term deposits; 2) credit operations, understood as those obtained from domestic or foreign loans and financing; 3) credit operations or contributions provided by federal, state, or municipal governments; 4) issuance or endorsement of mortgage bonds, including legally permitted rural credit bonds; and 5) other types of funding permitted by the Brazilian Central Bank.

The development banks played a key role in medium- and long-term financing of production activities. This included onlending of foreign funds, with the BNDES being the principal long-term financier for small and medium-sized companies at the beginning of the 1970s, providing subsidized loans to the private sector.

Beginning with the series of drastic increases in international oil prices, which hit Brazil particularly hard in 1973 and 1978, along with the resulting problems on the external front, the country's financing process was characterized by several difficulties. The need to honor foreign commitments through expansion of the domestic debt severely hindered the government's ability to finance new investments.

Especially in the second half of the 1970s, the need to obtain funding to pay interest and amortize the principal of Brazil's foreign debt led the government to keep domestic interest rates high. Thus, it became significantly advantageous for international companies and for Brazilian banks to take out huge loans overseas. The rising inflow of dollars, far exceeding immediate needs, drastically increased the economy's degree of liquidity. This meant the government had to issue public bonds, thereby increasing both domestic and foreign debt.

During this period, there was a change in the profile of financing in Brazil. The trend was for the government to invest less and less and for foreign capital to pick up the slack. This process became exhausted with the foreign debt crisis and the steep rise in domestic inflation as the 1980s got underway. The latter period, known as the lost decade, was marked by repeated attempts to manage these problems, mainly trying to curb inflation through a series of economic stabilization plans that proved unsuccessful.

In this context, two important changes took place at the beginning of the 1990s. The first, which is the focus of this study, is characterized by the search for new forms of financing on the part of major Brazilian companies. These new forms, which feature low levels of risk, are exemplified by the issue of depository receipts (DRs) on the international financial market. This decreases the dependency of Brazilian companies on funds available at home, which are in short supply, unstable, and very expensive due to the long period of recession the country experienced in recent years past. It is worth noting that, with publication of Annex V to Central Bank Resolution 1289 of 1992, Brazilian companies can now sell their shares overseas by issuing DRs. The second change that came about was the manner in which small and medium-sized companies began to finance their activities.

It cannot be denied that the BNDES continued to play a fundamental role in this area, though new financing avenues have been opened up in recent years. Commercial banks, which are able to obtain funding both inside and outside Brazil, have adopted a new strategic vision and have begun to diversify their investments. This process has included buying up and giving a new lease on life to small and medium-sized companies.

The role of these banks has gone beyond simple onlending of funds obtained from loans and financing. Now these institutions invest directly in companies, acquiring shares that range from small purchases of capital stock to outright control of major concerns.

Moreover, commercial banks have started to play an increasingly important role in channeling foreign funds to Brazilian companies. The World Bank (IBRD), which provides capital to BNDES for onlending to the Brazilian market in the form of financing, has begun to allow commercial banks to act as intermediaries in this type of transaction as well.

Another relevant factor in this setting of changes is the presence of a new funding agent, the Privatization Funds, which in 1994 accounted for 5 percent of total foreign funding.

This work studies the foreign sources of Brazil's financing on the basis of an analysis of recent history. Analysis is focused on the inflow of foreign funding, showing the legislative restrictions for foreign investment in Brazil and the modifications implemented in recent years.

Concrete examples of major companies, such as Aracruz Celulose (a huge pulp and paper concern) in the private sector and mining giant Vale do Rio Doce in the state-owned sector, clearly illustrate this shift in position. Aracruz pioneered in accessing the DR market, while Vale do Rio Doce inaugurated a new era in obtaining funding on the international market by issuing debentures.

The first part of this study is devoted to describing the means of obtaining funding in Brazil from 1970 onward, furnishing data on the variation in gross savings and the breakdown thereof in recent years, as well as its impact on the level of fixed gross capital formation.

The second part sets out some of the instruments through which funds available in the economy become accessible to investors. It also shows the trading volumes of these securities on the Brazilian market.

The third and final part of this study deals with financing provided by foreign capital. It shows the main channels for inflow of these funds into Brazil and the recent history of the country's macroeconomic environment with its effects on foreign funding.

Recent History of Investment In Brazil

The level of investment in an economy can be measured by gross capital formation in a certain period, which is equivalent to the variation of fixed capital[1] plus variation in inventories.[2] To achieve equilibrium, investments should be equal to savings, which can be divided into domestic and foreign.

Domestic savings are comprised of public savings, represented by the surplus of current revenues[3] over current expenses,[4] and private savings, which correspond to the portion of net income of families, enterprises, and institutions not spent on consumption.

Foreign savings[5] means how much foreign funds have been absorbed by the country. The balance thereof is expressed by current account deficits in the balance of trade or services. The balance of foreign savings is therefore the difference between investments and domestic savings.

When government revenues are not sufficient to cover its expenses, a budget deficit occurs, and the government savings balance is negative. In order for this not to lead to a drop in the rate of gross capital formation,[6] either private or foreign savings have to be increased.

Gross capital formation (GCF) decreased as a percentage of Brazilian gross domestic product (GDP) from 1981 to 1984; it rose during the period from 1984 to 1989 and dropped again until the beginning of the 1990s, as shown in Figure 1. The share of government savings in gross capital formation was negative for a full decade, from 1982 to 1992 (see Table 1). If public savings are analyzed as a percentage of GDP, one can see that this relation has been on a downward trend since 1977, with temporary growth recoveries in 1979 and 1985, as shown in Figure 2.[7] Contrary to what happened in the previous decade, when public savings reached as high as 6.35 percent of GDP, between 1980 and 1993 this ratio failed even to pass the mark of 1.1 percent of GDP. Such behavior can be explained by the domestic and foreign crisis Brazil underwent during this period, when the

Figure 1.
Gross Capital Formation

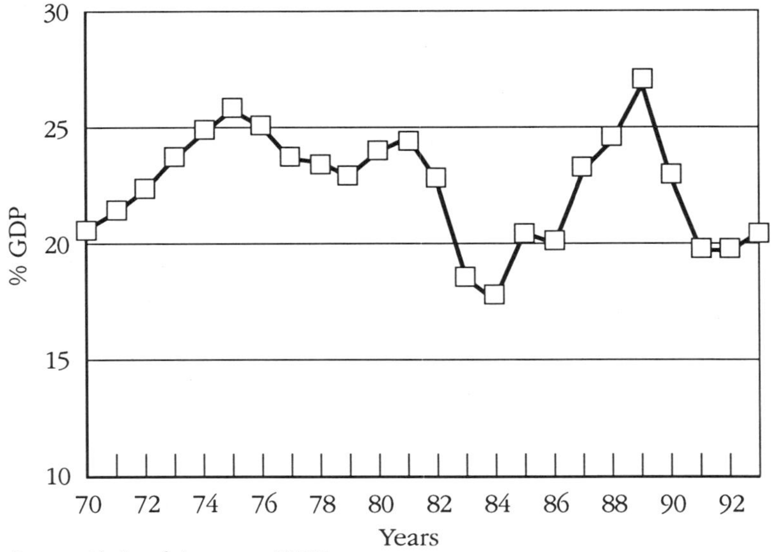

Source: National Accounts, IBGE.

Table 1.
Government Savings

	% GCF
1970	21.21
1971	22.40
1972	22.28
1973	23.04
1974	14.83
1975	11.99
1976	15.75
1977	15.18
1978	9.08
1979	10.05
1980	3.73
1981	4.55
1982	-1.59
1983	-8.02
1984	-17.83
1985	-42.28
1986	-37.11
1987	-27.50
1988	-55.01
1989	-80.80
1990	-47.97
1991	-1.98
1992	-24.45
1993	1.34

Source: IBGE.
GCF means Gross Capital Formation.

Figure 2.
Government Savings

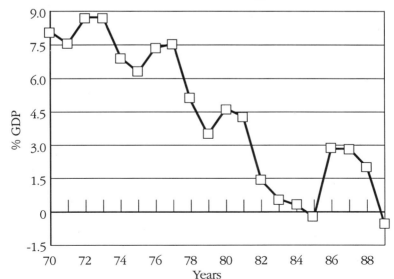

Source: Carneiro and Werneck 1992.

government was obliged to reallocate savings in an attempt to bring about foreign and domestic adjustments.[8]

The external shocks suffered by Brazil in the 1970s called for a process of adjusting domestic demand, which began in the middle of that decade. The second oil crisis, which led to the doubling of prices at the beginning of the 1980s and an increase in international interest rates, hindered the adjustment process underway. Decreased international liquidity caused a shortage of foreign funds, which were important to Brazil both in terms of making the domestic adjustment feasible and in rolling over foreign debts. The resulting recession meant a drop of around 10 percent in the country's industrial output in 1981.[9] The economic policy adopted in 1981 and 1982 was based on controlling domestic absorption. This involved an attempt to reduce the need to take out foreign loans. A drop in domestic demand would reduce imports and make exporting more attractive. The need for foreign capital, however, would only be reduced if the policy adopted caused a recession less than required to decrease the GDP to the same extent. The measures taken by the government included controlling public spending, freeing up interest rates of commercial and investment banks (except for exports and agriculture), and limiting credit expansion to 5 percent for commercial/investment banks and 15 percent for Banco do Brasil. This led to a severe liquidity squeeze.

Table 2.
Breakdown of Savings (% GDP)

	Public	Private	Foreign
1970	8.13	11.10	1.32
1971	7.57	11.03	2.66
1972	8.69	9.98	2.53
1973	8.69	11.35	2.01
1974	6.91	10.95	6.45
1975	6.32	14.22	5.16
1976	7.33	11.80	3.91
1977	7.58	12.17	2.28
1978	5.05	14.50	3.47
1979	3.47	14.85	4.80
1980	4.67	13.22	5.45
1981	4.28	14.36	4.44
1982	1.40	13.90	5.79
1983	0.62	12.70	3.37
1984	0.34	15.42	-0.02
1985	-0.22	19.31	0.11
1986	2.90	14.23	1.97
1987	2.87	18.95	0.49
1988	2.09	22.00	-1.28
1989	-0.52	25.61	-0.23

Source: Carneiro and Werneck, Text for Discussion n° 283, Economics Dept. PUC-RJ.

Mexico declared a moratorium in August 1982, making the debt crisis worse. This set of factors made it unfeasible to keep the Brazilian economy growing at high rates.[10] The exchange rate crisis that began in 1982 made it impossible to expand the debt to finance servicing of the debt itself. Thus, measured in net terms, Brazil was a net exporter of funds for a certain period. The means employed to finance this transfer of funds was the issuance of domestic debt instruments, in the form of net placement of government bonds. This led to a drastic drop in disposable income for the public sector and public savings. Private domestic savings and, in certain years, foreign savings were responsible for not letting the rate of gross capital formation fall below 17.6 percent of GDP (Table 3). Even so, as shown in Table 4, economic growth measured by annual real GDP increases fell from an average of 8.4 percent between 1970 and 1980 to 1.5 percent between 1980 and 1990.

It is interesting to note that gross domestic savings and foreign savings had opposite trends from 1980 to 1989: while one was on the increase, the other headed downward, and vice-versa (see Figure 3).[11] From 1970 to 1984, the drop in public savings was offset by the increase in foreign savings. The

Table 3. Gross Capital Formation		Table 4. Real GDP Growth	
	% GDP		%
1970	20.57	1970	7.75
1971	21.31	1971	11.41
1972	22.22	1972	11.95
1973	23.58	1973	13.94
1974	24.70	1974	8.25
1975	25.77	1975	5.12
1976	25.02	1976	10.17
1977	23.56	1977	4.93
1978	23.51	1978	4.93
1979	22.88	1979	6.77
1980	24.00	1980	9.11
1981	24.46	1981	-4.30
1982	22.63	1982	0.80
1983	18.38	1983	-2.90
1984	17.63	1984	5.40
1985	20.39	1985	7.80
1986	20.04	1986	7.50
1987	23.17	1987	3.50
1988	24.32	1988	-0.10
1989	26.86	1989	3.20
1990	22.90	1990	-4.40
1991	19.62	1991	0.20
1992	19.60	1992	-0.80
1993	20.38	1993	4.10

Source: National Accounts, IBGE.   Source: IBGE.

Figure 3.
Domestic and Foreign Savings (% GDP)

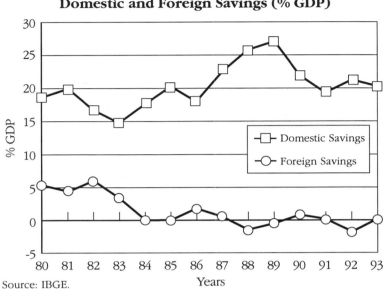

Source: IBGE.

Figure 4.
Breakdown of Savings

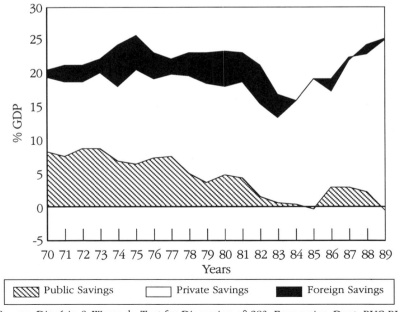

Source: Dionísio & Werneck, Text for Discussion n° 283, Economics Dept. PUC-RJ.

latter, in turn, dropped until 1989, when an upswing is noted more than proportional in private savings. This upswing was stimulated by the high level of domestic interest rates. Figure 4 shows the savings profile from 1970 to 1989.

Both domestic and foreign savings made financial resources available on the market for Brazilian companies through a set of instruments differentiated by built-in interest rates, type of applicable regulations, and other aspects.

From 1970 to 1980, the average rate of foreign savings represented 3.6 percent of GDP, private savings reached 12.3 percent, and public savings, 6.8 percent. Brazil grew by an average of 7 percent per year. Over the course of the 1980s, however, although the average rate of private savings increased to 15.7 percent, foreign savings dropped to 1.5 percent, and public savings fell significantly, averaging 1.4 percent.[12] It was therefore to be expected that growth levels would not repeat the same performance as in the previous decade.

Figure 4 shows private savings reaching high levels in 1989 compared to the average for the previous decade, while at the same time public savings fell to levels well below those observed in the preceding years.

Today, expectations are that domestic savings will hold steady. They may even rise to higher levels as the economic stabilization program under implementation in Brazil consolidates and matures. Nevertheless, it is not safe to depend on such growth as the sole source of financing. This is

Table 5.
Public Accounts — Uses and Sources
Cash Flows at Prices of Last Month Considered R$ millions (*)

Itemizations	1991 Jan-Dec	1992 Jan-Dec	1993 Jan-Dec	1994 Jan-Nov	1994 Jan-Dec	1995 Jan-Nov
Uses (1+2+3)	**(2)**	**37**	**616**	**(10,120)**	**(9,186)**	**19,478**
Primary Result (1)	(4)	(36)	(1,194)	(26,463)	(27,555)	(6,365)
Interest on Domestic Debt (2)	—	50	1,109	12,730	14,626	22,517
Interest on Foreign Debt (3)	2	23	701	3,613	3,743	3,326
Sources (4+5+6)	**(1)**	**36**	**617**	**(10,119)**	**(9,185)**	**19,477**
Domestic Financing (4)	(4)	53	627	(10,019)	(15,704)	34,765
Foreign Financing (5)	—	(60)	(1,096)	(17,802)	(15,713)	(12,801)
Currency Issued (6)	3	43	1,086	17,702	22,232	(2,487)
Operating Results (**)	**(2)**	**36**	**617**	**(10,119)**	**(9,186)**	**19,477**

(*) Amounts prior to July 1994 translated by URV as of June 30, 1994.
(**) Deflator: INPC (centered) - Índice Nacional de Preços ao Consumidor.

because the prospects for public savings are very limited due to the subsequent public deficits (Table 5), which make foreign savings a fundamental instrument for Brazil to return to the high growth levels experienced in the past.

It is important to note that, if compared to public and private savings, foreign savings in the 1970s, although modest, were much higher than at the end of the 1980s. Foreign savings, therefore, are clearly an important factor for Brazil's economic growth, in light of the average GDP growth of 9 percent per year during the 1970s.

The next section will analyze some of the more recent instruments for foreign funding currently in use in Brazil.

Foreign Funding

The Main Inflow Channels

In recent years, there has been not just a change in the profile of financing for the Brazilian economy, with gradual replacement of public domestic funds for foreign private funds, but also a shift in the instruments used to obtain such funding.

New foreign funding instruments have arisen recently, such as export securities (regulated in 1991) and depository receipts (DRs — regulated in 1992), among others. Parallel to this, certain channels already existing on the market have become popular as sources of foreign financing. Such is the case with debenture issues, direct investments, and portfolio investments.

It is not due to any other reason that the available information on funding on the international market is scarce. Owing to the low volumes handled in certain types of transactions through 1988, the Brazilian Central Bank (BACEN) did not even consolidate the respective data.

This section describes some of the funding instruments used in Brazil.

Debentures. Debentures are a long-term credit instrument and hardly a new one on the financial market. The Brazilian Corporation Law[13] increased the types of securities that could be issued, altered the limits of such issues, and provided that the Brazilian equivalent of the U.S. Securities and Exchange Commission — the CVM — would be responsible for laying down the rules and controlling compliance therewith. However, only after the creation of the Brazilian Debentures System (SND) in 1987 did the country witness implementation of a secondary debentures market and invigoration of the primary market for these securities.

According to the legislation, whenever tangible guarantees are posted, debenture issues are not to exceed 80 percent of the value of the encumbered assets, and they cannot exceed 70 percent of the book value of the company's total assets, the deduction of the amount of debt guaranteed by tangible rights being due, in the case of debentures with floating guarantees.

Brazilian companies may issue debentures overseas as long as prior approval is obtained from the Central Bank. As for their maturities, they may vary from case to case with no restriction being specified on the legislation.

Resolution 1833 of the Brazilian Monetary Council (CMN), dated June 26, 1991, allowed issue of debentures with an exchange rate variation clause linked to future export revenues of the issuing company. Such securities are to be issued for a minimum period of three years.

The public offering of debentures, which was in the incipient stages until 1980, considerably increased through 1982, the year in which funding through this type of instrument totaled US$1.9 billion. During the period from 1984 to 1987, both the number of debentures offered and the total value thereof decreased considerably. In 1987 only US$22 million was obtained in funding through debenture issues.

A recovery took place in 1988, and debenture issues resulted in market funding of around US$3.2 billion. However, it is interesting to note that the total amount increased tremendously, exceeding the amount raised in 1982 by fully 68 percent, while the number of debenture offers was a mere 12 percent of the debentures offered in the latter year (see Figure 5 and Table 6).

In fact, beginning in 1981 with the liquidity squeeze brought on by the credit restrictions imposed by the government, one of the forms encountered to get around these limitations was the issue of debentures. Financial institutions were unable to supply credit, but they could buy debentures from companies, thus meeting the existing demand. This is the reason the debentures market heated up.

Little by little, the liquidity squeeze was lifted, and the market returned to normal conditions. In 1987, when the SND was created and the secondary debentures market was implemented, offer of these securities picked up once again.

Commercial Paper. The commercial paper type of security in Brazil is a short-term promissory note, issued by a publicly traded company, with fixed maturity that may be different in each case. It is normally used by large companies. It was regulated in June 1990 by CMN Resolution 1723. Issues of promissory notes are restricted to companies whose stockholders' equity is not less than 10 billion BTNF[14] units, and authorization has to be obtained from the CVM. CMN Resolution 1734 of July 31, 1990, permits obtention of funding on foreign markets through the issue of commercial paper.

Use of this type of security was on the rise until 1991, when it attained a volume of US$1,783 million, approximately three times the volume obtained the previous year, representing 15 percent of the total foreign funding for that year. Beginning in 1991, use of this instrument declined somewhat, and by 1995 commercial paper only accounted for US$381 million of all foreign funding, just 1 percent of that total (Table 9).

Export Securities. Export securities are a funding instrument, regulated by CMN Resolution 1834 of June 26, 1991, that allows Brazilian

Figure 5.
Public Debenture Offerings

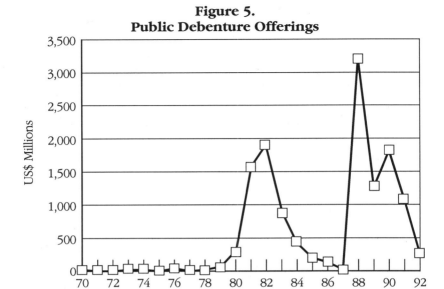

Source: CVM - Comissão de Valores Mobiliários.

Table 6.
Public Debenture Offerings

Year	Quantity	Value (US$ millions)
1970	6	19
1071	1	0
1972	0	0
1973	5	20
1974	3	15
1975	2	12
1976	3	37
1977	2	7
1978	2	25
1979	7	74
1980	44	304
1981	185	1,587
1982	256	1,901
1983	162	876
1984	89	427
1985	53	209
1986	10	133
1987	7	22
1988	30	3,198
1989	41	1,261
1990	83	1,796
1991	74	1,064
1992	39	245

Source: CVM - Comissão de Valores Mobiliários.

Figure 6.
Commercial Paper

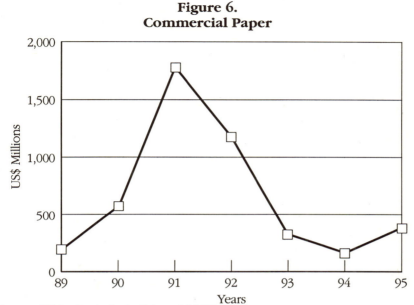

Source: CVM - Comissão de Valores Mobiliários.

companies to obtain currency from foreign markets. These securities are linked to the borrower's exports or to those of its related companies.[15] Based on the export contract, the exporter issues a security with a minimum term of one year in order to seek financing on the international market. In 1991, this instrument allowed Brazilian companies to obtain total funding of US$278 million. In 1993, the total jumped to around US$675 million but has dropped off since then, as shown in Figure 7. From 1994 onward, there is a slight recovery in terms of volume of funding obtained, although expectations are that, in light of the operational complexity of this mechanism, it will only become important again if other funding mechanisms become scarce.

Depository Receipts. Depository receipts are certificates representing shares, issued overseas and backed up by securities; they can be traded in other countries. Applicable rules are contained in Resolution 1927, issued on May 18, 1992, by the CMN. The DRs basically can be traded in three different ways: between institutional investors overseas, by foreign stock exchanges, and by over-the-counter (OTC) markets abroad. Generically, they are classified as sponsored and unsponsored DR facilities. What distinguishes between a sponsored and an unsponsored facility is the responsibility for covering the costs of issuing and placing this type of paper on the market.

Figure 7.
Export Securities

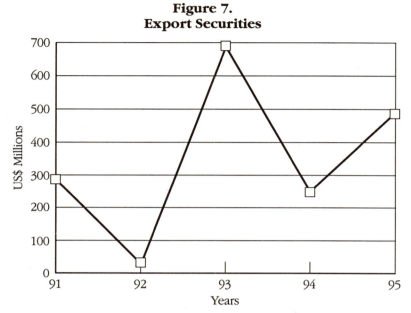

Source: Banco Central do Brasil, Boletim, Vol 32 n° 1, January 1996.

These instruments are regulated in the following ways:[16]

Level 1. The program is initiated by the issuing company and is the easiest manner for a company to control the issue of its ADRs in the United States. It does not involve issuing new shares but rather trading shares previously issued.

The operation is intermediated by a bank, though there is no registration with the SEC[17] and therefore no stock market trading. Level 1 DRs are traded over-the-counter and placed with qualified institutional investors (pension funds, insurance companies or portfolio managers handling equities of at least US$100 million).

Level 2. Level 2 ADR facility is begun by the issuing company to correspond to the demand by U.S. investors for its shares. Like the level 1 ADRs, they involve trading of existing issues, not new ones, and as with level 1, a bank has to serve as a go-between. In this case, however, SEC registration is mandatory. This makes such operations more attractive to U.S. investors, since allowing them to be traded on U.S. stock exchanges increases their liquidity.

Level 3. Level 3 securities are similar to level 2 ADRs, except that the paper trade corresponds to new primary issues exclusively placed for overseas trading. Accordingly, capital increase is involved.

Rule 144-A. Rule 144-A regulates private placements in the United States, allowing previously qualified buyers to purchase securities that adhere to the rules of other markets. As this type is aimed at institutional investors, there are no requirements to adapt to SEC accounting standards, but at the same time, it allows for the issuing company to obtain new funding.

Regulation S. This modus operandi allows sales of publicly traded companies to investors in off-shore markets at significant discount rates and without SEC registration.

The facilities encountered in the U.S. securities market, where individuals and companies alike can trade freely in ADRs, coupled with the prohibition against foreign financial institutions to serve as underwriters in Brazil, has stimulated the issue of ADRs to a considerable extent.

If, on one hand, the issue of these securities by Brazilian companies constitutes an important capitalization alternative, on the other hand, the growing volume of shares blocked to back up issue of these DRs naturally means that trading volumes of Brazilian stock exchanges has been decreasing.[18]

This transfer of liquid assets overseas represents a problem, to the extent that the already relatively small Brazilian equities market (compared with other developing countries) will tend to shrink even more.

However, solving this problem does not mean creating difficulties for access to this type of instrument. Instead, it means searching for means of decreasing the level of red tape for foreigners to invest in Brazil and expanding the Brazilian capital markets.

Circular Letter 2445, issued on March 21, 1994, created a specific code to cover such operations. From then on, considering the data available through March 1995, the inflow under this heading totaled US$1,765 million versus a total outflow (transfers or remittances from Brazil) of US$1,095 million. Thus, the positive balance was around US$670 million, as shown in Table 7.

Foreign Exchange Contract Advance (ACC). The foreign exchange contract advance or ACC consists of partial or total advance in Brazilian currency (Reais) equivalent to the amount of foreign currency purchased on a term basis from the exporters by the bank. The objective is to provide funds to the exporter in order to finance production and sale of the merchandise to be exported. The ACC can be separated into two phases. The first phase involves the bank granting the advance up to 180 days prior to shipment of the goods. In the second phase, when the goods are ready for shipment, an advance for foreign exchange delivery (ACE) can be requested up to 60 days after shipment. Quite frequently, the ACC is used to make financial gains, since it is possible to get money at low cost and obtain substantial yields on the Brazilian financial market, due to interest rate arbitrage. The legislation governing this type of funding has been altered to prevent the misuse of the ACC funds from happening. Circular 2334 of June 30, 1994, forbids extension of the maximum period for foreign exchange advance to the one set out in the contract. Advanced export payments are defined as funds invested in foreign currency upon settlement of export exchange contracts prior to shipment of the goods.

Table 7.
Depository Receipts
(US$ Millions)

Period	Inflow	Outflow	Balance
1994	**1,221.5**	**873.0**	**348.5**
March	15.8	19.8	(4.0)
April	47.3	38.4	8.9
May	71.4	26.0	45.4
June	144.8	113.2	31.6
July	77.3	127.2	(49.9)
August	87.1	139.4	(52.3)
September	460.9	241.5	219.4
October	111.5	73.5	38.0
November	119.6	46.2	73.4
December	85.8	47.8	38.0
1995	**543.2**	**222.3**	**320.9**
January	285.0	66.7	218.3
February	141.6	50.9	90.7
March	116.6	104.7	11.9

Source: Banco Central do Brasil, Análise do Mercado de Câmbio, first quarter-1995.

Table 8 shows that the ACC and ACE totals rose from around US$27 billion in 1990 to US$31.6 billion in 1994. In 1993, the ACCs and ACEs represented 83.1 percent of total exports contracted by Brazil. This share dropped to 74.2 percent in 1994. The amount of these contracts in the first quarter of 1994 was around 46 percent below that observed in the same quarter of 1993. This decline was a consequence of the restrictions imposed by the government on such contracts at the end of the year. These restrictions explain the significant increase noted in the early payment mechanism, the manner in which exporters get around mandatory payments imposed on contracts for future settlement.

Operation 63. This type of operation, regulated by Resolution 63 of August 17, 1967, allows Brazilian financial institutions authorized to conduct foreign exchange transactions to obtain foreign funding for onlending to Brazilian companies and banks for a minimum period of 90 days.

These are loans offered on the domestic market, using funds obtained overseas through the issue of bonds and eurobonds with rates and terms matched to the international funding terms.

Table 8.
Foreign Exchange Contracts Export, Prepaid, ACC & ACE

Period	Export	Prepaid	%	ACC & ACE	%	Prepaid + ACC & ACE	%
1990	33,410	2,215	5.9	26,993	80.8	29,207	87.4
1991	34,504	3,251	8.6	27,422	79.5	30,674	88.9
1992	39,369	4,578	12.1	31,633	80.4	36,211	92.0
1993	37,807	3,965	10.5	31,413	83.1	35,378	93.6
Jan	2,867	516	18.0	2,223	77.5	2,739	95.5
Feb	2,519	275	10.9	2,124	84.3	2,399	95.2
Mar	2,868	334	11.6	2,436	84.9	2,770	96.6
April	3,061	397	13.0	2,543	83.1	2,940	96.0
May	3,187	360	11.3	2,699	84.7	3,059	96.0
June	2,953	291	9.9	2,453	83.1	2,744	92.9
July	3,071	240	7.8	2,585	84.2	2,825	92.0
Aug	3,435	371	10.8	2,930	85.3	3,301	96.1
Sept	3,217	416	12.9	2,570	79.9	2,986	92.8
Oct	3,437	182	5.3	2,909	84.6	3,091	89.9
Nov	3,405	246	7.2	2,880	84.6	3,126	91.8
Dec	3,787	337	8.9	3,061	80.8	3,398	89.7
1994	42,562	5,784	13.6	31,599	74.2	37,383	87.8
Jan	4,030	568	14.1	3,284	81.5	3,852	95.6
Feb	3,166	346	10.9	2,626	82.9	2,972	93.9
Mar	4,003	531	13.3	3,175	79.3	3,706	92.6
April	4,115	624	15.2	3,266	79.4	3,890	94.5
May	4,614	637	13.8	3,561	77.2	4,198	91.0
June	4,168	454	10.9	3,322	79.7	3,776	90.6
July	2,752	351	12.8	2,166	78.7	2,517	91.5
Aug	3,361	350	10.4	2,630	78.3	2,980	88.7
Sept	3,499	326	9.3	2,786	79.6	3,112	88.9
Oct	3,234	425	13.1	2,306	71.3	2,731	84.4
Nov	2,539	537	21.2	1,117	44.0	1,654	65.1
Dec	3,081	635	20.6	1,360	44.1	1,995	64.8

Source: Brazilian Central Bank.

This instrument functions as a loan in dollars, restated according to the variation in the commercial dollar rate and subject to international interest rates.

In the cash loan mode, Resolution 63 was an important channel for Brazil to obtain foreign funding in the 1970s.

In the present decade, its use expanded, rising from US$6 million in 1990 to US$856 million in 1992 (Figure 8). In 1995, after two years of decline, total funding obtained through this instrument amounted to US$817 million. Even so, it still represented just 2 percent of Brazil's total foreign funding for that year.

FIRCE Communiqué No. 10. This type of operation regulates direct operations between Brazilian non-financial companies and foreign institutions (both financial and non-financial). There are no securities issued under this modus operandi.

The funding obtained through this instrument jumped from US$110 million in 1989 to US$2.27 billion in 1995, which represents growth of 1,837 percent. It should be noted, however, that its relative share of total funding did not even pass the 4 percent level last year.

Leasing. Generically, leasing is an operation based on an agreement whereby the lessor grants third parties the right to use an asset for a determined period. The agreement or contract can include an option to renew or purchase at the end of the lease period.

This type of instrument provides full financing on a long-term basis for any new or used property or asset.

Figure 8.
Resolution 63

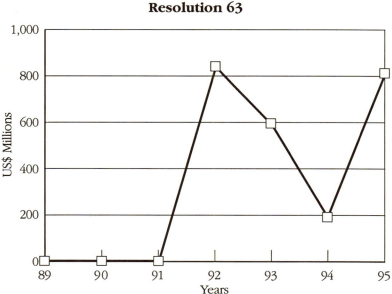

Source: Banco Central do Brasil.

Figure 9.
FIRCE Communique N° 10

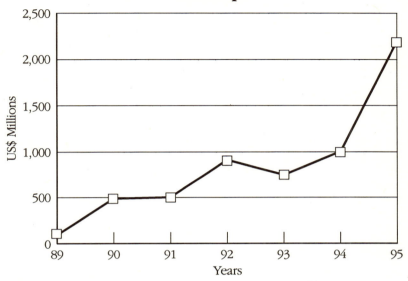

Source: Banco Central do Brasil, Boletim, Vol. 32 n° 1, January 1996.

Figure 10.
Leasing

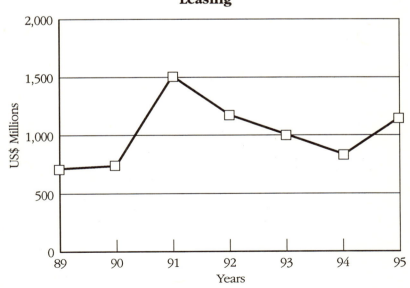

Source: Banco Central do Brasil, Boletim, Vol. 32 n° 1, January 1996.

In international leasing, a company located overseas leases an asset to a Brazilian company for at least two years. The value of the lease is FOB, and international interest rates are normally charged.

The volume of funding obtained through leasing increased by 58.5 percent between 1989 and 1995, although its share of total funding was substantially reduced, going down from 17 to 2 percent during this six-year period.

Access to the International Market in the 1990s

Macroeconomic instability prevailed in 1991. While on the foreign front the Persian Gulf War caused major swings on international financial markets, domestically the situation was hardly different, aggravated by the country's still weak economic conditions. The failure of Collor Plan I, with prices rising, and the Central Bank facing difficulties in decreasing the system liquidity by placing bonds were the main factors indicating the need for structural changes to be made in the economy.

This led to the implementation of Collor Plan II, basically character-ized by a total revamping of Brazil's financial system. The principal measures of this new plan were the following:

- ending the overnight market;
- ending short-term investment funds, which were replaced by a new form of investment called the Financial Investment Funds (FAF). These funds became the main buyers of federal public bonds, and the monetary policy adopted by the Central Bank was conditioned to the net worth of the FAF, thereby reducing its room for maneuver; and
- creating the Reference Rate (TR), a sort of managed prime rate that theoretically reflected the level of interest charged in the system, though in fact only reflected interest rates on CDs. The rise in inflation again meant that in some months the TR was negative in real terms. As one of its functions was to serve as an instrument to restate passbook savings accounts and the FAF, devaluation against inflation frequently caused investments to get out of such assets.

This set of factors, coupled with the release of funds blocked by Collor Plan I, caused concern in government circles regarding a possible consump-tion explosion. Thus, the monetary policy adopted by the Central Bank for the second half of 1991 was focused on administering short-term demand. There was a substantial increase in interest rates, from 0.4 percent (in real terms) per month (4.9 percent per year) in August to 4 percent per month (60 percent per year) in September, in order to try and rein in consumption and inflation.

A medium-sized devaluation of Brazil's currency was made on the last day of September 1991 in order to correct the deteriorating exchange rate situation, which was then hampering exports. This measure, along with a rise in utility rates — by approximately 20 percent — resulted in a jump in inflation rates (8 percent more per month). To counter pessimistic expectations and prevent increased pressure on consumption after release of the blocked New Cruzados (the currency at the time), the last quarter of 1991 was marked by major upward pressure on interest rates.

Despite the growing attractiveness of fixed income assets, which resulted from high interest rates, the stock market managed to continue playing a key role. The incentive for foreign fund investors to place their bets here, the initial success of the Privatization Program, the renewed dialogue between the government and foreign creditors, and implementation of strict fixed income market rules proved strong enough to bolster the local stock market. Both Brazilian and foreign investors were attracted, although trading volumes involving the latter were still fairly negligible.

Some of the measures adopted by the Brazilian government during the course of 1991 were important for the national economy to become more closely aligned with the international financial community. This process created room for obtaining foreign funding and room for foreign investors to become interested in Brazil again. Such measures included payment of overdue interest and institution of separate negotiations for the private sector's foreign debt and for the restructured public debt. In this manner, funds received from overseas grew by approximately 117 percent between 1990 and 1991 (Table 9).

Traditional credit operations, largely involving loans on the Brazilian financial market, gave way to foreign financing operations. This shift was brought on by the high domestic interest rates and the excessive weight of the country's tax burden (one of the world's highest). The first steps were taken in terms of operations involving export securities. Export securities closed out 1991 with a total volume of US$278 million. Funding through commercial paper rose significantly, shooting up threefold from US$568 million in 1990 to US$1.8 billion in 1991, and accounted for 15 percent of all foreign sources in that year.

Issues of bonds and notes likewise virtually tripled, rising from US$540 million in 1990 to US$1.5 billion in 1991.

The attractiveness of the country's domestic interest rates compared with the international market, the good prospects apparently ahead for the Brazilian economy as perceived at the beginning of 1992, and the rise in the cost of domestic credit quickened the pace of inflowing funds during 1992. This came in the form of direct investments, export contract advances, and issue of securities overseas. To control the monetary impact of this movement, the Central Bank made full use of the domestic public debt. Even so, market concern regarding the government's capacity to roll over this debt, coupled with the strangulation of the country's fiscal situation, pressured interest rates even further for acquisition of such bonds.

At the same time as the increase in the inflow of foreign funds in 1992 permitted accumulation of reserves topping US$20 billion, the government's fiscal performance grew worse in light of the strategy and type of instrument used to sterilize the impact of these funds on the economy.

Table 9.
Funding From Foreign Sources
US$ Millions

	1989	1990	1991	1992	1993	1994	1995
Total	4,201	5,367	11,627	17,911	32,667	43,073	53,447
Investments	333	688	1,455	5,308	15,928	27,214	28,010
Portfolio Investments	149	171	760	3,683	14,971	21,600	22,559
Direct Investments	184	517	695	1,625	877	2,241	3,285
Fixed Income Funds	0	0	0	0	80	1,434	211
Privatization Funds	0	0	0	0	0	1,939	1,955
Cash Loans	361	1,045	4,408	7,979	11,031	8,756	15,883
Firce Com. no. 10	110	405	470	922	769	1,053	2,170
Resolution 63	0	0	6	856	597	201	817
Resolution no. 2148 (1)	0	0	0	0	0	0	1,067
Commercial Paper	198	586	1,783	1,190	338	182	381
Bond & Notes	0	540	1,507	4,833	7,598	5,961	9,650
Expert Securities	0	0	278	30	675	261	494
Renewals	53	0	364	148	1,054	1,098	1,304
Financing	2,786	2,882	4,160	2,332	3,282	4,353	4,443
Leasing & Rental	721	752	1,519	1,173	1,005	842	1,143
Prepaid Exports	0	0	85	1,119	1,421	1,908	3,968

(1) Direct Rural Financing
Source: Banco Central do Brasil, Boletim, Vol 32 n° 1, January 1996.

The rise in the inflow of funds was facilitated further by continuity on the government's part of the process of easing up on rules for entry of foreign capital, which was begun in 1991. Several measures were approved that facilitated Brazilian credit overseas and opened the economy up to foreign capital. Among these are the following, by way of example: 1) carrying out of floating rate market interbank operations through the Central Bank System (SISBACEN); 2) ending the requirement for the Central Bank to approve foreign exchange contracts in advance, thus decreasing the level of red tape involved in such operations; 3) permitting interest rate swaps; and 4) integrating Brazilian stock exchanges with those of Argentina and Uruguay, as part of the MERCOSUR[19] pact. For instance, in April 1992, Cia. Vale do Rio Doce (CVRD) issued notes overseas in the amount of

US$150 million, with maturity starting in April 1995 and at the lowest rate of interest achieved until then by a Brazilian company.

In spite of indications that foreign funding in 1992 would increase even more than the 117 percent posted in 1991, the political crisis that dominated the national scene since May led to decreasing inflows in the second half of 1992. Nonetheless, there was a real increase of 54 percent during 1992. Although interest rate policy caused one of the worst recessions in the country's history, it certainly drew investor attention to the fixed income market. Investment funds also performed outstandingly. In order to encourage even more foreign funds to come into Brazil in the form of collective investments, the National Monetary Council (CMN) authorized foreign capital funds in July 1992 to carry out operations on the futures and options markets. This action reduced the vulnerability of these portfolios to market swings. Parallel to this, the Central Bank authorized functioning of commodities funds to stimulate the futures market. From September to December 1992, the yields of these funds were similar to those of the fixed income funds (158 percent) and even exceeded them in volume terms. The stock market absorbed the impacts of the crisis in a negative manner. Real losses for the year were 10 percent. The trading values of shares were below their book values, thus hindering this form of funding by the productive sector.

During 1993, despite macroeconomic instability and record-level inflation (2,568 percent for the year), foreign capital continued pouring into Brazil through various routes. This inflow put pressure on the monetary base and required the Central Bank to adopt a stricter strategy in order to prevent the currency from veering out of control. These funds were basically characterized by their volatility and were considered speculative capital; they were characterized as such because they belonged to investors that, given international liquidity, were attracted by the advantages Brazil offered in relation to other countries. The speculative nature of this capital can be noted, for example, by the fact that of the US$16.5 billion in foreign investments made in Brazil in 1993, no less than US$9.3 billion (approximately 56 percent) returned overseas (Table 10).

Despite the ebbs and flows of foreign investment during the year, as the political crisis unraveled, the total balance was up 83 percent from the previous year. Inasmuch as trading volumes were still rather insignificant, the stock markets reflected the impact of foreign operations, and the stock exchanges were the most profitable investment of 1993.

Regarding funding through issue of securities overseas, Brazilian companies obtained funding of approximately US$11 billion, an increase of around 38 percent in relation to the previous year. Low international interest rates — a factor that increased the acceptance of Brazilian securities overseas — and the possibility of arbitrage between domestic and foreign interest rates were the main causes of this increase in demand.

During the first half of 1993, real domestic interest rates were reduced, pursuant to orders by the country's new president, Itamar Franco. The objective of this policy was to make growth possible in spite of inflation. This approach caused conflicts between the Franco administration and the

Table 10.
Capital Movement

Itemization	1988	1989	1990	1991	1992	1993	1994
Investments	2,269	125	0	170	2,972	6,170	8,131
Brazilian	-175	-553	-731	-1,015	-137	-1,094	-1,037
Foreign	2,444	678	731	1,185	3,109	7,264	9,168
Inflows	2,734	1,409	1,028	1,508	5,437	16,546	27,648
Return	290	731	297	323	2,328	9,282	18,480
Financing	-424	-1,431	-3,512	-4,076	-3,425	-2,908	-1,907
Disbursements	2,631	2,257	2,662	2,125	1,608	1,435	2,389
Amortization Paid	3,055	3,688	6,174	6,201	5,033	4,343	4,296
Cash Loans	-595	-1,495	-968	2,368	5,761	5,865	3,712
Disbursements	4,100	706	911	3,997	7,875	10,790	10,417
Amortization Paid	4,695	2,201	1,879	1,629	2,114	4,295	6,705
Total	1,250	-3,341	-4,480	-1,538	5,308	9,127	9,936
Inflows	9,467	4,375	4,602	7,649	14,947	29,227	40,923
Outflows	8,217	7,716	9,082	9.187	9,639	20,100	30,987

Source: Banco Central do Brasil, Boletim, Vol. 30 n°7, July 1994 and Vol. 32 n°1, January 1996.

Figure 11.
Capital Movement

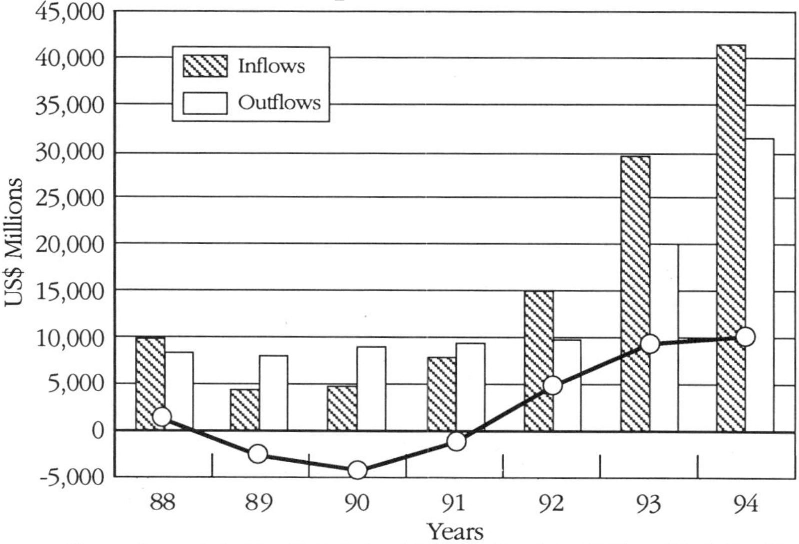

Source: Banco Central do Brasil, Boletim, Vol. 30 n°7, July 1994 and Vol. 32 n°1, January 1996.

Central Bank (BACEN), which did not support such measures. Thus, in the second half of the year, the administration's economic team was changed, and its enhanced synergy with the president allowed the return to a policy of higher real interest rates.

The new rise in interest rates caught the attention of foreign investors, and the BACEN was forced to adopt restrictive measures to neutralize this effect. Circular 2344 of July 21, 1993, reduced the sold position of foreign currencies of the country's banks by one-half, which allowed the market (non-financial system) to have a greater supply of local currency; at the same time, according to circular 2344, the bought position of foreign currencies in the financial institutions was boosted fivefold, which allowed the banks to keep a higher level of foreign currencies that otherwise would have been transferred to the Central Bank and, thus, consequently reduced the cost of international reserves for the monetary authority.

Moreover, the government began to levy the financial operations tax (IOF) on foreign capital. The government's objective was not just to discourage speculative foreign capital but also to bring more money into its budget.

Beginning in September, the Central Bank altered the strategy of its monetary policy, acting simultaneously on both the exchange and interest rates markets. There was convergence of parallel, floating, and commercial exchange rates so that the premium among these markets was reduced to virtually zero. In order to prevent speculations regarding exchange rates and prices, the government once again increased real interest rates, this time to 2.5 percent per month in October, the highest level of the year.

In December 1993, a new economic plan was announced, basically involving a fiscal adjustment and the adoption of the Unit of Real Value (URV), a shadow currency linked to the dollar. Subsequently, the URV was to be transformed into a full-fledged dollar-linked currency, with the purpose of freeing the Brazilian economy from indexation once and for all.

The first half of 1994 was a transition period from an unstable economy to an economic order in which the inflation process was finally under control. Naturally, that first semester was marked by various types of speculation and consequent market volatility.

With the implementation of the Real Plan in July, there was a sharp drop in inflation and a rise in consumption, caused by years of pent-up demand. To adjust for this imbalance, the government jacked up interest rates again and adopted credit restrictions.

The growing differential between domestic and foreign interest rates, as well as optimistic expectations in relation to the Real Plan, caused foreign capital to continue pouring in. This led to substantial increases in trading volumes on the country's stock exchanges. Significant real gains were posted (the São Paulo stock exchange index IBOVESPA rose 14.16 percent, the national index ISENN rose 39.41 percent, and the Rio de Janeiro stock exchange index IBV rose 15.73 percent).

To prevent excessive capital inflows from pressuring the monetary base, the government adopted a series of measures to restrict foreign capital in October 1994. This caused the stock market profitability to decrease from that point onward.

The drop-off in foreign capital inflows was reduced considerably at the end of 1994 also as a reflection of the Mexican crisis. Even so, foreign funding rose by a healthy 32 percent in Brazil in comparison with 1993. Of the total funding, which amounted to US$32 billion, 50 percent moved into portfolio investments.

The consolidation of the Real Economic Stabilization Plan over the course of 1995 required a somewhat restrictive monetary policy. This resulted in even higher interest rates than those in effect the previous year (33.36 percent versus 24.17 percent recorded in 1994, as measured by the Getúlio Vargas Foundation's General Price Index for Domestic Demand IGP-DI/FGV).

If, on one hand, the exchange rate valuation (appreciation of the Real in relation to the dollar) at the end of 1994 and beginning of 1995 caused successive trade deficits, on the other hand, the Mexican crisis and the subsequent devaluation of the peso caused foreign investors to flee.

These factors resulted in a reduction in the country's international reserves, leading the government to review the foreign capital restrictions adopted at the end of 1994. With the end of the Mexican crisis, this situation was turned around, and the massive entry of capital forced the BACEN to take more of a hands-on approach to prevent devaluation of the Real. Thus, 1995 wound up with total foreign funding of US$53.5 billion, almost one-quarter (24 percent) more than that of the previous year.

It is interesting to note that, besides the rise in the volume of foreign funding, there has been a change in the profile thereof over the course of the present decade. In 1989, the financing category accounted for 66 percent of the total funding obtained on the international market. This share decreased as the 1990s progressed, and by 1995 it was just 8 percent. By the same token, portfolio investments experienced the opposite, shooting up from 4 percent of the total in 1989 to 42 percent of the total in 1995.

In studying capital movements (see Table 10), it is evident that 1989 and 1990 were critical years in terms of funding for Brazil. Besides the fact that capital inflows were much lower than posted in 1988, down 54 and 51 percent, respectively, the volume of capital outflows was quite high as well. In 1990, outflows were 11 percent higher than those of 1988. Accordingly, in 1989 and 1990, Brazil posted considerable deficits in terms of its capital flows with other countries. In 1991, there was a 66 percent increase of incoming funds, although this was still not sufficient to yield a positive balance. The inflows continued to grow steadily, rising by an impressive 95 percent in 1992, 96 percent in 1993, and 39 percent in 1994. On the other hand, outflows were minimal, just 5 percent increase in 1992, which made the balance initially jump up by an astonishing 445 percent. Later, outflows picked up considerably once again (106 percent in 1993 and 56 percent in 1994), and the balance continued to rise steadily albeit at decreasing rates (80 percent in 1993 and 4 percent in 1994).

As shown in Table 11 below, to a great extent 1994 funding was comprised of funds coming in under the Annex IV mode. Thus, investments made by foreign institutional investors represented 85.82 percent of the total.

Table 11.
Funding Breakdown

	Amount (US$ Thousand)	%
Annex II (mil)	647,700	2.75
Fixed Income Fund	2,186,905	9.27
Annex IV	20,240,741	85.82
Others	509,875	2.16
Total	23,585,222	100.00

Source: ANBID Report, August 1994.

Foreign Exchange Liberalization Process

A Brief History

Brazil's capacity to use foreign funds to finance its economic development is, in fact, quite limited. Subject to outside restrictions, the Brazilian economy endured a long period of highly restrictive exchange rate legislation. By and large, the government sought first to encourage the inflow of capital and then to prevent it from leaving.

The limitations imposed on the outflow of funds, while necessary from a situational point of view, wound up impeding — along with a series of other factors — the access of the Brazilian economy to funds on the international market. Institutional hurdles (mainly red tape), combined with the low level of internationalization of the Brazilian economy, led foreign savings to have only a small share in the breakdown of total savings in the national economy (Figure 4).

Undoubtedly, during the boom years of the 1970s, in the midst of the so-called "economic miracle," there was relatively greater use of foreign savings in Brazil, mainly in the form of financing (66 percent). Nonetheless, the average rate of foreign savings as a portion of GDP was just 3.64 percent during the period. At the time it was relatively easy to obtain foreign financing due to the abundance of funds available and the low interest rates charged. Access to the international financial market during the early 1970s was achieved mainly by state-owned enterprises, backed up by guarantees from the national treasury. This profile changed drastically in the 1990s, and one of the indicators of such a move — although partial — is the breakdown between public and private sector debt of the total foreign debt for the period 1990-1994.[20] Private companies (financial and otherwise) upped their share from 23.3 percent in 1990 to 41.4 percent in 1994, and parallel to this, there was an 8.8 percent decline in the volume of funds obtained by the public sector and a 111 percent increase by the private sector (Table 12).

In the 1980s, a series of factors led to a situation where it was virtually impossible for Brazil to obtain credit on the international market. Among the main reasons was the oil crisis of 1978, the sharp reduction in the supply of foreign credit, and the subsequent rise in international interest rates. Added to these factors were the domestic economic crisis resulting from exhaustion of the development cycle of the 1970s and the country's difficulty in generating enough earnings to pay off its foreign debt commitments.

In this context of cash shortages, it was necessary to choose between sending foreign money back overseas to pay for imports (mainly oil) or to finance tourism expenses in foreign currency or even other activities relatively less important to the national economy. The result was that the 1980s were noteworthy for fairly restrictive exchange rate legislation. Accumulating foreign exchange earnings, under slogans such as "Exporting is What is Important" with a whole slew of export incentives, including exchange facilities, was the overriding objective for the period. As a result of such strategy, the average level of US$6.37 billion in the 1970s grew to US$8.14 billion in the following decade (Table 13).

Restrictions on the free flow of capital appear to have created a certain aversion in Brazilian society to transactions involving capital. This aversion got to the point where virtually any remittance overseas was considered "illegal" or at least illegitimate. Traces of flexibility only emerged toward the end of the 1980s with the strong neoliberal current then sweeping the political scene.

In the 1990s, the situation was substantially altered, and the country once again recovered its capacity to obtain funding on the international market. This came about for various reasons. On the external front, emphasis was placed on the huge supply of low-cost capital and the

Table 12.
Total Foreign Debt (US$ Millions)

	1990	1991	1992	1993	1994
Public Sector (*)	94,679	94,627	93,437	90,614	86,330
Private Sector	28,760	29,283	42,512	55,046	60,965

(*) Non-financial public sector, excl. Petrobrás & CVRD.
Source: Banco Central do Brasil, Boletim, Vol. 31 n° 12, December 1995.

Table 13.
International Reserves (US$ Billions)

Year	Cash (*)	International Liquidity (**)
1971	—	1.7
1972	—	4.0
1973	—	6.4
1974	—	5.3
1975	—	4.0
1976	—	6.5
1977	—	7.3
1978	—	11.9
1979	—	9.7
1980	—	6.9
1981	—	7.5
1982	—	4.0
1983	(1.6)	4.6
1984	7.5	12.0
1985	7.7	10.5
1986	4.6	6.5
1987	4.4	7.5
1988	5.4	9.1
1989	7.3	9.7
1990	8.8	10.0
1991	8.6	9.4
1992	19.0	23.8
1993	25.9	32.2
1994	36.5	35.4
1995	50.4	51.2

(*) Brazilian Central Bank Operational Concept, considering readily available assets.
(**) In addition to "cash," aggregate assets representative of export notes and medium-
    and long-term assets.
Source: Brazilian Central Bank.

recommencement of negotiations involving the foreign debts of several
Latin American countries, including Brazil. Domestically, a major role was
played by the stabilization effort culminating in the Real Plan, which
significantly reduced the degree of uncertainty of the national economy.
Contributing too were the easing up on foreign exchange curbs and the
invigoration of privatization programs, which made Brazil once again
attractive to foreign investors. Also worthy of mention is the major role
played by monetary policy from 1994 onward, with very high interest rates
(10 percent per month) compared with those on the international market
(10 percent per year).

In the context of this new macroeconomic environment, it became
desirable for exchange rate legislation to be adapted to the new times. As
early as 1988, creation of the floating rate exchange market via Resolution
1552 was an important step in this direction. When the floating rate market
was launched at the beginning of 1989, it allowed the formal market to
incorporate foreign exchange operations previously carried out on the

"parallel market" (black market), which used to be much more rewarding because the difference between the black market and the official rate was so great (100 percent) due to prohibitive regulations.

Since then, the floating rate market has been used to guarantee greater flexibility to foreign exchange operations. For more than a year now, there have been virtually no quantitative limitations to earnings leaving Brazil, either for tourism expenses or for one-way transfers. Nevertheless, all foreign currency transactions have to be recorded each day on the Central Bank's Electronic System for Control and Registration of Operations (SISBACEN), for purposes of Brazilian Central Bank control.

So far, the 1990s most certainly have been marked by heightened national consciousness regarding the inevitability of Brazil being a full-fledged partner in the international financial market. It is becoming increasingly clear among Brazilian society that the country must obtain foreign funding to finance economic growth above the current rate of 4 to 5 percent per annum, which is insufficient to absorb the growth of the labor force.

It is worth noting that, given the series of massive deficits in Brazil's public accounts (Table 5), the government's capacity to serve as the locomotive of national development is clearly compromised. To make matters worse, there are no prospects for short- or even medium-term recovery. Fiscal reform, which is indispensable to the government to recover its financing capacity, has encountered strong resistance in the Congress. It appears highly unlikely that there will be any changes in the constitutional text in the current term of the administration of President Fernando Henrique Cardoso (1995-1998).

Concerning private domestic savings, it is worth pointing out that, although on the rise, it did not suffice to offset the reduction in public savings and foreign savings during the 1980s.

There can be no doubt that Brazil has taken the neoliberal medicine prescribed for developing countries after the foreign debt crisis. The choices of stability, economic liberalization, and easing up on foreign exchange policy are the basic characteristics of the neoliberal model. Such fundamentals, put into practice ever since the administration of Fernando Collor de Mello (1990-1992), certainly have contributed to foreign capital returning to Brazil.

Naturally, this process takes a long time and, as such, has been relatively continuous in the first half of this decade. After Collor was impeached on corruption charges and removed from office, his vice-president Itamar Franco took over. Later, the Real Plan became the campaign priority of then-candidate Fernando Henrique Cardoso (Franco's former finance minister), who managed to get elected in the first round of voting by a substantial margin over the second-placed candidate.

Despite the clear-cut objective of foreign exchange liberalization, the stabilization exercise paradoxically has led Brazil to the need to impose situational controls over the inflow of foreign capital. It even has led to altering the country's foreign exchange legislation. Such a contingency has wound up impacting the expectations of the international investors and, therefore, their decision as to whether or not to invest in Brazil. Prospects for altering the rules according to the immediate needs of the economic circumstances have served to ward off more long-term foreign investment that, when all is said and done, is what Brazil actually needs more than anything else.

From the second half of 1994, the flow of capital to and from Brazil has been characterized by a tremendous volatility, times of relative scarcity and others of abundance of foreign money. Thus, as price stabilization has been the government's number one priority, the treatment dealt out to foreign capital has been at the mercy of this project. In the two years of the Real Plan, restrictive measures were followed just a few months later by a sharp degree of flexibility. The need for short-term fine-tuning of capital flows from month to month has not allowed Brazil to enact a long-term strategic approach to foreign capital investments.

At any rate, important changes have been implemented since 1990, with a view to creating conditions for obtaining foreign funding in a stable economic environment.

From an institutional standpoint, it is worth pointing out the transformations involving the Brazilian Central Bank (BACEN), particularly its Foreign Capital Department (FIRCE). This department is currently undertaking a foreign capital census project in order to be able to treat foreign capital as economic information only and no longer to deal with it as a regulatory agency. This project is expected to be concluded in the near future.

Mention should further be made of the revision of Law 4131 (September 3, 1962), which regulates foreign investment in Brazil. This revision was recently undertaken by the government (executive and legislative branches) together with representatives of foreign investors. This gave rise to Bill 4647, presently making its way through Congress. The objective of this law would be to simplify and cut excessive red tape from operations involving foreign investment. This, it is hoped, will eliminate the principal distortions existing in foreign currency legislation.

Various initiatives also have been taken to lower the existing barriers to commercial and financial flows between Brazil and its foreign partners. Among these are the following:

- reducing the tax burden on profit remittances and dividends, from 25 to 15 percent;
- continuing the Brazilian privatization program, allowing foreign investors to bid at privatization auctions as well and to use foreign debt conversion instruments in the process;
- creating MERCOSUR, the Southern Cone Common Market, with Brazil playing a major role;
- Brazil returning successfully to the international market, featuring issues of securities totaling over US$17 billion since 1990;

- negotiating the foreign debt on a long-term basis, culminating in April 1994 with the exchange of debt for bonds under the scope of the Brady Plan;
- foreign investors with access to Brazilian equities portfolios, with gross inflows of over US$35 billion (US$13.6 billion net) beginning in 1990; and, moreover,
- Brazilian companies being allowed to issue depository receipts and thus place their shares on international markets.

Capital Inflows as from the Real Plan

The third phase of the Economic Stabilization Plan first implemented by the Itamar Franco administration on July 1, 1993, essentially was based on a restrictive monetary policy, with quarterly local currency issue targets and fiscal and exchange rate policies subordinate to such targets. Prior definition of currency issue limits subsequently was abandoned, with the Real Plan essentially anchored on changes in the face value of the currency.

The exchange rate policy defined by the government's economic team initially revolved around a so-called "exchange band," which was asymmetrical. It involved setting a maximum price for sale of the dollar (US$1.00 = R$1.00) and flexibility in terms of the purchase price as long as it was below the sale price.

With the implementation of the new economic standard, the Real (R$), expectations were that the drastic reduction in the profitability of financial investments would lead to a strong remonetization process, benefiting the local currency but with risk, which could not be considered negligible, of a boom in consumption. This led the economic team to keep interest rates extremely high on the financial market.

The difference between domestic and foreign interest rates, which was essentially attractive to international capital, chiefly stimulated the inflow of foreign currency to Brazil. Running against this was the major appreciation in terms of the exchange rate in the first half of 1994. This made it possible to avoid compromising the monetary issue targets, albeit with serious consequences for the national balance of trade.

The potentially negative effects on exports were undeniable, but policymakers counted on the capacity of part of the export sector to absorb the exchange rate valuation, at least for a certain period. Contributing to the government's viewpoint were positive structural factors such as the rise in productivity. Situational factors, such as the possibility of financing with foreign funds from foreign exchange contract advances (ACC) and advanced export payments at relatively low costs, also contributed to counterbalance the negative effects on exports of an appreciated local currency. Yet another aid to total exports was the rise in prices of Brazil's main commodities on the international market.

With the strong real exchange rate valuation in the months of July and August (12 and 22 percent, respectively, based on the Wholesale Price Index for Domestic Demand) compared to June 1994, there was an effective reduction in the inflow of dollars. Among the factors explaining the reduction in capital inflows during this period were indefinition in relation to changes in exchange rate policy, as well as the uncertain climate on the political scene, with the possibility of Workers Party (PT) candidate Luís Inácio "Lula" da Silva winning the election. The problem with the latter candidate was that he had no explicit commitment to continue with the stabilization plan begun during the term of his opponent, Fernando Henrique Cardoso, as finance minister.

The net results of the flow in foreign currency reflected the economic and political environment for the period: As seen in Table 14, the monthly balance of foreign exchange contracts both for commercial and financial transactions — which ranged from US$1.5 to US$3.6 billion between January and June 1994 — amounted to only US$337 million in the months of July and August 1994.

From 1992 through the first half of 1994, although the foreign exchange balance was significantly higher than after introduction of the new economic standard in July 1994, around US$16 to US$20 billion, the Central Bank bought excess dollars in the market in order to sustain the exchange rate. From the moment BACEN stopped buying excess foreign currency (July 1994), banks began accumulating such a huge stock of dollars that the successive positive foreign exchange balances only pressured the dollar downward in Brazilian currency. Thus, with lower balances, the market became saturated, with no more room to absorb the inflow of dollars.

In an attempt to provide long-term equilibrium to the foreign exchange market — both the floating and free exchange rates — the Central Bank had three alternative or complementary economic policy options: 1) stimulating domestic demand for the dollar by loosening rules, 2) playing an active role again in the exchange rate market as a direct buyer, and 3) preventing excess foreign capital inflows through imposition of restrictive measures.

By and large, the return of the Central Bank to the exchange rate market as a major dollar consumer would not seem to be a feasible proposition, given the basic premise of its need to maintain rigid control over expansion of the monetary base. By buying dollars, the institution would be injecting Reais (plural of Real) into the economy, which as a general rule would be completely contrary to its attempt to maintain monetary control, as it would require placement of public bonds to reduce excess liquidity in the market. On one hand, this would cause a rise in domestic public debt. On the other hand, it would put upward pressure on interest rates, creating further attraction to foreign capital. In this sense, it was to be expected that the government would adopt measures to discourage the attraction of foreign capital and encourage increased

Table 14.
Foreign Exchange Contracts — Commercial & Financial
Operations with Customers (US$ Millions)

Month	Year	Commercial			Financial			Total Balance
		Export	Import	Bal. 1	Purchase	Sale	Bal. 2	(1+2)
	1987	26,581	13,226	13,355	2,400	11,644	(9,244)	4,111
	1988	33,465	14,359	19,106	2,585	15,528	(12,943)	6,163
	1989	34,295	17,553	16,742	2,314	16,897	(14,583)	2,159
	1990	33,421	19,552	13,869	3,635	14,183	(10,548)	3,321
	1991	34,504	19,755	14,749	7,699	15,514	(7,815)	6,934
	1992	39,557	18,819	20,738	16,351	16,506	(155)	20,583
	1993	37,806	21,842	15,964	29,757	27,805	1,952	17,916
	1994	42,551	25,823	16,728	39,926	40,170	(244)	16,484
Jan		4,030	1,848	2,182	3,338	2,187	1,151	3,333
Feb		3,164	1,571	1,593	3,522	2,678	844	2,437
Mar		4,002	1,780	2,222	3,078	3,717	(639)	1,583
Apr		4,111	1,499	2,612	2,537	2,493	44	2,656
May		4,611	1,594	3,017	2,790	2,182	608	3,625
Jun		4,168	1,644	2,524	3,211	2,922	289	2,813
Jul		2,752	1,878	874	2,341	2,878	(537)	337
Aug		3,361	2,334	1,027	3,074	3,795	(721)	306
Sep		3,499	2,458	1,041	3,712	4,909	(1,197)	(156)
Oct		3,233	2,477	756	4,561	4,355	206	962
Nov		2,539	3,157	(618)	3,815	3,420	395	(223)
Dec		3,081	3,583	(502)	3,948	4,630	(682)	(1,184)
	1995	53,142	41,547	11,595	48,324	47,748	576	12,171
Jan		3,969	3,501	468	2,689	4,610	(1,921)	(1,453)
Feb		4,460	3,223	1,237	1,899	3,323	(1,424)	(187)
Mar		4,322	3,993	330	2,235	6,606	(4,371)	(4,041)
Apr		4,059	3,631	429	2,842	3,533	(691)	(262)
May		5,082	3,585	1,497	4,119	3,215	905	2,401
Jun		4,365	4,205	161	4,348	4,346	3	163
Jul		4,945	3,068	1,876	5,174	3,067	2,107	3,983
Aug		4,714	3,383	1,331	7,607	3,592	4,015	5,346
Sep		4,462	3,040	1,422	3,915	3,842	73	1,494
Oct		4,394	3,443	951	5,279	3,299	1,980	2,931
Nov		4,394	3,391	1,004	4,435	3,652	782	1,786
Dec		3,974	3,120	855	5,241	4,665	575	1,430
Jan	1996	4,117	3,107	1,010	5,524	3,275	2,249	3,259

Sources: Brazilian Central Bank; ANECC - Associaçao Nacional de Empresas Credenciadas em Câmbio.

domestic demand for foreign currency, thus reducing the need for intervention by BACEN as a main player on the foreign exchange market.

Accordingly, on August 31, 1994, the National Monetary Council (CMN) decided to adopt a series of measures generally aimed at stimulating demand for the dollar. Such measures essentially involved the following: 1) allowing all foreign currency operations (buying and selling) to be contracted for prompt or future settlement (CMN Resolution 2104), 2) altering item 4 of FIRCE Communiqué 25 to permit financing of imports for 360-day periods to involve the full amount of the product traded (BACEN Circular Letter 2486), and 3) making early settlement of foreign currency loans and import financing optional (CMN Resolution 2105).

Specifically in relation to the floating exchange rate market, the alterations made involved increasing the limit for nonfinancial companies to make remittances for Brazilian investments overseas from US$1 million to US$5 million, as well as allowing corporate entities with head offices in Brazil to purchase real estate overseas, which was previously restricted to individuals (BACEN Circular 2472).

Other measures taken to stimulate demand for the dollar were the Central Bank's decisions to reduce import duties and to modify regulations on the floating (Circular 2478) and free (Circular 2479) markets on September 12, 1994. The aim of these actions was to permit future settlement of exchange rate financial operations.

On the floating exchange rate market, the alteration made could lead, in principle, to increased demand for the dollar. It made it possible to contract foreign currency in advance for payment of overseas obligations (health care, for example) to be made at a future date. The expectation was that there would be an earlier foreign exchange contracting by potential customers seeking to take advantage of the low price of foreign currency.

Stimulating demand for the dollar appeared to be the most attractive approach in the view of the monetary authorities. However, such an option did not prove to be effective on a short-term basis.

With Circular 2480, likewise issued on September 12, 1994, the Central Bank appeared to have found a means of returning to direct intervention on the market, though without pressuring expansion of the monetary base, in the case of purchasing dollars, or fostering major speculative purchase or sell movements. This is because, according to the circular in question, transactions involving foreign currency purchase and sale options by BACEN on the interbank market would as a general rule (though not necessarily) be carried out through foreign exchange auctions over the SISBACEN. Thus, whenever it deemed it necessary to buy or sell foreign currency in smaller amounts than it would if the operation were handled through an auction, the Central Bank could do so without even appearing in the market. It could simply use a single bank of its choice.

Since July 1994, with the introduction of the Real, a series of restrictive measures were adopted in order to prevent a massive inflow of dollars from constituting additional pressure on the monetary base and conversely giving rise to an appreciation of the Real above the desired level. At the same time, the significant reduction in the costs of imports left no doubts as to the genuine possibility of trade deficits and, therefore, current account deficits as well. Nevertheless, it was expected that the short-term capital flows by way of investments and loans, abundant and relatively cheap, would be maintained, in light of President Cardoso's high level of credibility and the attractiveness of domestic interest rates. There were expectations that the terms of funding obtained overseas would be lengthened and direct investments by non-Brazilian residents would increase.

With the exchange rate crisis that erupted at the end of 1994, foreign investors shied away from Latin America, including, of course, Brazil. This made capital flows negative from November 1994 onward. Funding on the international market became a trickier task, with greater selectivity on the part of borrowers and increase in the interest rates charged.

In the Brazilian financial sector, the tax burden and liquidity squeeze imposed by the Central Bank caused major difficulties. From the implementation of the Real onward, this segment of the national economy endured a series of measures reducing liquidity. It even led several major institutions to bankruptcy. Central Bank Circular 2511, which came out on December 2, 1994, made this situation even worse as far as the financial sector was concerned. From then on, any operation involving funding and investments between a financial institution and a nonfinancial company meant a compulsory deposit had to be made. The possibilities of funding overseas and then onlending without being subject to the compulsory deposit were reduced to practically zero. With this, the difficulties of obtaining credit from the financial market were increased to a significant degree.

The most relevant effect of the Mexican crisis on Brazil's foreign exchange policy was in fact that of indicating the danger of letting foreign accounts get out of control. The problem was that such accounts were basically financed by short-term capital precisely at a time when there was a crisis of confidence on the part of international investors.

It was for no other reason that in January 1995, a series of foreign exchange regulations were eased in order to encourage foreign capital inflows once again. By and large, the measures adopted were aimed at stimulating export financing. This contributed to reducing the perverse effects of exchange rate valuation on the competitiveness of Brazilian exports in the international marketplace.

On January 11, 1995, the Central Bank issued Circular 2534, which eliminated the 15 percent compulsory deposit on the ACCs (foreign exchange contract advances). BACEN issued Circular 2538 on January 24, revoking Circular 2438 of June 30, 1994, that had permitted early export payments of at least 720 days and Circular 2490 of October 19, 1994, that had suspended early payment of long-term export exchange contracts indefinitely. It re-established the minimum 360-day period for early export payment, as provided in Circular 1979 of June 27, 1991.

Finally, on January 25, 1995, the Central Bank issued Circular 2539, which expanded the short-term advance export payment period to a maximum of 360 days, regardless of whether the contract was matched to

Figure 15.
Foreign Funding — Terms and Costs[1]

Itemization	1994				1995			
	I	II	III	IV	I	II	III	IV
Total								
No. of Issues	79	57	39	55	42	57	91	68
Amount (US$ millions)	5,019	1,587	1,813	3,153	1,496	3,325	5,866	3,630
Average Period (year)	4	6	5	5	5	4	4	6
Spread (basic points)[2]	497	453	526	490	436	527	529	517
Total Cost (% per year)	10.17	10.91	12.05	11.87	11.82	11.27	11.26	10.92
Private Financial Sector (Onlending)								
No. of Issues	56	21	17	35	16	28	54	35
Amount (US$ millions)	3,987	596	948	2,500	517	1,696	3,076	2,278
Average Period (year)	4	5	4	4	4	3	4	6
Spread (basic points)[2]	499	478	535	486	437	561	549	495
Total Cost (% per year)	10.11	10.86	11.96	12.04	11.84	11.68	11.40	10.67
Non-Financial Private Sector (Onlending)								
No. of Issues	23	34	22	20	26	27	34	32
Amount (US$ millions)	1,032	673	865	653	979	585	1,814	1,017
Average Period (year)	6	7	6	7	6	6	5	7
Spread (basic points)[2]	488	476	517	507	435	505	563	568
Total Cost (% per year)	10.42	11.26	12.14	11.22	11.81	11.28	11.66	11.48
Public Sector								
No. of Issues	—	2	—	—	—	2	3	1
Amount (US$ millions)	—	318	—	—	—	1,044	976	335
Average Period (year)	—	8	—	—	—	3	3	5
Spread (basic points)[2]	—	358	—	—	—	483	404	513
Total Costs (% per year)	—	10.26	—	—	—	10.60	10.09	10.94

1 = Funding Operations authorized by Central Bank through issue of securities on international market, in the form of Floating Rate Notes, Fixed Rate Notes, Floating Rate Certificates of Deposit, and publicly or privately placed bonds.
2 = Difference between cost of operation and quotation of similar term U.S. Treasury Notes.
Source: Banco Central do Brasil, Boletim, Vol. 32 n° 2, February 1996.

an ACC. Only the differentiation per type of product was maintained. According to Circular 2493 of October 19, 1994, early export payments were permitted no more than 300 days in advance, depending on the size of the exporting company and the type of product. Circular 2539 also extended the periods of the ACCs from 30 to 60 days, in the case of products with domestic supply problems, and to 180 days for other products.

All of these measures undoubtedly impacted the contracting of export exchange. In December 1994, the average daily export exchange operations contracted totaled US$139.92 million. Imports in the same month were clipping along at a daily pace of US$165.08 million, which meant a daily negative balance in commercial transactions of US$25.16 million. In January 1995, on the other hand, the average daily export exchange operations contracted rose to US$180.38 million, while imports dropped to US$159.14 per day, increasing the average daily commercial transactions total to US$21.24 million. It is important to point out that the average daily export exchange operations contracted in 1995 (US$215.75 million) were over 50 percent higher than those in December 1994.

In light of the new international macroeconomic environment, the Central Bank took measures to prevent impairment of foreign accounts. These measures came in the form of Communiqué 4479 on March 6, 1995, which instituted the exchange rate band system, with the dollar varying from between R$0.86 and R$0.90 until May 1995 and from R$0.86 to R$0.98 thereafter.

Notwithstanding the Central Bank's signaling that a transition exchange rate of R$0.93 would be put into effect, the prior announcement of widening the exchange rate band after May 2, 1995, caused widespread market uncertainty. The upshot was a series of speculative moves that were unprecedented after the Real was implemented. This speculative activity required the BACEN to intervene numerous times (around 40 in just a single week) in the exchange rate market in order to sustain the established band.

In December 1994, Brazil's international reserves added up to US$38.8 billion, according to the international liquidity concept. This was proof of the maneuvering room the monetary authorities had to guarantee the value of the national currency. By and large, this meant that Brazil had sufficient reserves to guarantee 12 to 13 months of imports (considering the average for the period from February 1994 to January 1995). The limit considered reasonably safe is four months (US$11.5 billion).

In this context, the declining financial situation in Argentina, which largely resulted from foreign financing based on short-term capital, only served to strengthen the arguments of those pushing for adoption of additional measures to protect the Brazilian market against capital flight and to attract medium- and long-term capital to the Brazilian market, as well as direct foreign investments. These measures came on March 10, 1995, in order to make the Brazilian economy less vulnerable.

The overall objective of the economic team was to discourage demand for the dollar, increase capital inflows, and reduce the level of speculation in the financial system. The increase brought about in domestic interest rates also was used to achieve such goals.

In this sense, the rate of the financial operations tax (IOF) was reduced on the local currency equivalent of foreign money coming into Brazil — from 7 to 0 percent on cash loans, 9 to 5 percent on fixed income fund investments, and 1 to 0 percent for investments in bonds and marketable securities (Administrative Rule 95, issued by the Finance Ministry). Permission for early payment of cash loans and import financing was revoked by Resolution 2147. Minimum periods for certain operations were established — 24 months for foreign loans (Circular 2456) and 180 days, counting from the original maturity date, for renewals or extensions of foreign credit operations involving issue of securities overseas (Circular 2547). The limits of position purchased from banks were sharply reduced (from US$50 million to US$5 million on the free rate exchange market [Circular 2549] and from US$10 million to US$1 million on the floating rate market [Circular 2548]) for purposes of depositing the excess amount at the Central Bank. For those allowed to operate in the floating exchange rate market, the purchased position limit was reduced from US$1 million to US$500,000 (Circular 2548).

Finally, in order to make it absolutely clear that it would not permit any significant devaluation of the Real, the Central Bank issued Communiqué 4492. This revoked the earlier BACEN Communiqué 4479 that had established a new floating band for the dollar (R$0.88-0.93). The measures imposed were certainly strong and quite austere, even to the point of breaching commitments previously agreed upon.

During its first anniversary, the Real Plan began to undergo changes in at least two essential areas: 1) exchange rate policy and 2) the economy's indexation structure. The latter had, in fact, been forecast ever since the Plan's inception, when it limited the term for existence of the official inflation index (IPCr) to just one year.

On June 20, 1995, the number of dealers (institutions authorized to operate with the BACEN) was expanded from 20 to 60, and the spread auction was instituted. The latter permitted the Central Bank to take purchase and sale quotations at the same time from the dealers. This expanded its room for maneuvering so that, by negotiating at both ends, it could counteract speculative jolts. Upon announcing the exchange band system, the Central Bank spent a significant amount of its reserves in an attempt to contain market pressures that were severely testing the exchange band.

On June 22, 1995, Brazil's monetary authorities brought about the next-to-last rise in the exchange band (from R$0.88-0.93 to R$0.91-0.99). This affected appreciation of the Real considerably, mainly due to the country's declining balance of trade. Since November 1994, consecutive trade deficits were posted. These deficits came after the perverse effects of the choice made in October — to liberalize hastily, mainly by sharply reducing import duties, at the same time that Brazil's currency was kept strong — became all too evident.

The Brazilian government's foreign exchange policy over the course of the Real Plan was characterized by alternating restriction with stimulation insofar as flow of foreign capital was concerned. This stop-and-go policy was the means encountered by the monetary authorities to ease the impacts of the international macroeconomic environment on domestic price indices.

Given the high mobility of capital at the international level, the adoption of measures restricting the free flow of capital to and from Brazil frequently was required to assure continuity of the country's economic stabilization process. On several occasions, the performance of the foreign accounts likewise demanded adoption of such measures. Even so, it was desirable for such measures to be temporary and be tied in with controls over prices (tariffs rather than quantities/quotas). This was not always possible, however.

Beginning in July 1995, the massive inflow of capital made the adoption of harsh measures essential. Fortunately, the government hit on the right ones — tax control instruments. In August, through Administrative Rule 202, the Finance Ministry raised the IOF on the Brazilian currency equivalent of foreign money coming into Brazil — from 5 to 7 percent on fixed income fund investments, 0 to 5 percent on loans, and 0 to 5 percent on investments in bonds and marketable securities. Furthermore, Administrative Rule 202 extended the IOF (regulated by Decree 1591) at the rate of 7 percent to interbank operations carried out between foreign financial institutions and Brazilian banks authorized to handle foreign exchange operations, as well as on transactions whereby foreign residents make short-term funds available in Brazil (CC5 operations).

Subsequently, Finance Ministry Administrative Rule 228 of September 15, 1995, created different IOF rates for inflow of capital arising from loan operations in order to stimulate more long-term funding. Under this rule, the 5 percent rate began to apply only to loans with a minimum average term of two years, dropping for each additional year (three, four, and five years) to 4, 2, and 1 percent, respectively. Funding operations with minimum term of six years now incur zero IOF. Creating a scale for this tax has caused a difference not only in terms of quantity but also in quality, as it allows Brazil to indicate the type of capital it wants invested.

Such measures were responsible for reducing the net inflow of capital on the free rate market, despite the still considerable difference between domestic and foreign interest rates. Nonetheless, beginning in July 1995, the net monthly inflow of earnings into Brazil never dipped below US$1.4 billion, the level prevailing in the period immediately prior to the Real Plan.

In 1990 and 1991, the average monthly inflow was US$277 million and US$578 million, respectively. In the following years, these amounts increased fantastically. In 1992, the record net total of US$20.6 billion that entered Brazil made the monthly average work out to US$1.7 billion. In 1993, 1994, and 1995, although still high, the balances were on the downswing — US$1.5, US$1.3, and US$1 billion, respectively. In the second half of 1995 alone, the net total coming into Brazil was US$16.9 billion, of which US$9.5 billion (56 percent) arose from financial operations.

However, the make-up of capital during the second half of 1995 began to take on a different profile. As shown in Table 14, the major inflow of capital to Brazil beginning in the second half of 1995 is more balanced. It is being tugged by financial transactions (investments in the capital and financial markets, as well as loans) rather than by commercial transactions. Formerly, the latter were brutally stimulated by the automatic currency devaluations practiced.

In August 1995, the net inflow of capital was US$5.3 billion, US$4 billion resulting from financial transactions. In September, however, the respective amounts were reduced to US$1.5 billion and US$73 million. This was the worst foreign exchange balance from financial operations registered until January 1996.

The Central Bank's adoption of a new exchange band on January 30, 1996, (R$0.97-1.06 = US$1.00) did nothing to alter the course of the exchange rate policy. Since the introduction of the exchange bands mechanism in March 1995, Brazil's exchange rate policy has been characterized by a gradual devaluation of the Real, even in real terms. This has partially offset the trend for interest rates to go down as a result of the looser monetary policy during the period. The main instrument used by the BACEN was the establishment of smaller informal intervals for dollar variations known as mini-bands. These were backed up by purchase, sale, or spread auctions.

The need to ensure systematic exchange rate corrections, albeit without the automatic indexation characteristic of the pre-Real period, arose from the fact that Brazil still had to live with inflation higher than that of the United States. Price indices continued to rise by slight amounts each month. These rises could not be ignored, which made exchange rate devaluation fundamental to ensure solid performance of the country's commercial transactions. Over the course of 1995, monthly exchange rate variations ranged from a maximum of 5.29 percent in March to a minimum of 0.21 percent in September. The main reason for such variations was the awful performance of the balance of trade, which posted negative results during the entire first half, accumulating an annual deficit of around US$3.1 billion.

In January 1996, the net inflow of capital was US$3.3 billion. Of this total, US$2.2 billion or 67 percent involved financial transactions, marking the return of foreign investors to the Brazilian capital markets. The São Paulo stock exchange alone took in net investments of US$694.7 million in that month, an amount even higher than the total inflow posted in 1995 — US$512 million.

The surplus trend continued in February, leading the Central Bank to intervene on the purchase end in order to assure the recently established exchange rate band. In the first five days of February, no less than US$1.4 billion came into Brazil, 63 percent (US$854 million) from financial transactions. If this situation had not been altered, net inflows of approximately US$4.5 billion would have been posted by the end of that month.

To prevent such an inflow pressure, on February 9, the Central Bank published a series of measures more selective than restricting of capital inflows as such. The measures involved the following: 1) instituting the rate of 5 percent on privatization funds for foreign capital; 2) establishing new rules for investing funds obtained on the basis of Resolution 63/67 (basically, such funds are to be passed on to the final borrower or other financial institutions; now it is forbidden to invest them in Brazilian Treasury Bonds with dollar guarantee clauses); 3) altering the provisions of attachments I, II, III, and IV of Resolution 1289 (restricting the investment of foreign funds in privatization currencies); 4) increasing to 36 months the average period for amortizing foreign loan operations contracted, renewed, or extended; and 5) authorizing and regulating foreign capital investments in mutual investment funds for emerging enterprises.

The overriding motivating factor in the series of measures adopted was to encourage lengthening of the period of foreign capital investment in Brazil and reducing its volatility. The main reason for this was to prevent occurrences such as happened in Mexico, which faced a serious exchange rate crisis by being so dependent on short-term foreign capital to finance its current account deficit. The selectivity sought with the new rules should bring more peace to the exchange rate market without, however, compromising Brazil's foreign exchange flows.

Attractive Elements of Foreign Capital

In a modern capitalist economy, such as the United States, economic agents make medium- and long-term decisions and clinch deals based on their future expectations. To such end, the definition by the government of stable rules that assure contracts will not be broken is fundamental to guarantee an environment of minimum credibility. Systematic alterations in rules undoubtedly imply losses and negatively affect investment decisions, which by their nature tend to be more long term. This is perhaps the highest price paid for a stop-and-go policy, retreating and advancing, thus constantly changing the rules of the game on the external front.

By and large, the economic policy put into practice by the Cardoso administration is a provisory policy, in that it is based on nominal anchors. The objective is to guarantee in a low-inflation environment the time required for structural reforms to be approved by the Congress. The Real Plan's rationale, therefore, only makes sense with the implementation of such reforms, chief among which are those on the administrative, patrimonial, fiscal, social security, and land reform fronts. The latter is aimed at absorbing part of the unemployed masses in the cities and is not just a situational problem. On the contrary, it has profound roots in the techno-logical restructuring of industry, which is less and less labor-intensive.

One important means for inserting foreign capital into the Brazilian economy by way of direct investment certainly is related to patrimonial reform of the state. Increased participation by the Brazilian states in the privatization process has been identified as a way to improve budget performance. States need to dismantle their property structure and join the privatization bandwagon. The willingness demonstrated by the new crop of governors finally to resolve their states' long-standing cash shortages, including relief programs for state banks, would appear to buttress this argument.

Continuity of the Brazilian privatization program should open up more room for strategic partnerships with international capital. This will enable the privatized companies to enhance their competitiveness. The benefits to be reaped by Brazil from such partnerships, in both public and private sectors, derive from the possibility of harnessing both the technol-ogy ability and the connections with the international market so character-istic of the major multinationals.

Effective inflow of foreign funds in the form of direct investments in Brazil, however, probably will be conditioned to the reduction of the so-called Brazil risk. In light of the government's budget constraints — at federal, state, and municipal levels — public investment in basic infrastruc-ture (transportation, energy, communication, among other sectors) has become deficient, even to the point of discouraging new foreign companies from setting up business. Mainly based on the commercial facilities created in the MERCOSUR countries (Brazil, Paraguay, Argentina, and Uruguay), largely in relation to tariffs, the relative cost of the infrastructure components appears to have acquired added importance in the decision of foreign companies to choose one country over another for their new investments.

Accordingly, the general perception is that as long as structural reforms are not made, the overall macroeconomic balance will be unstable and therefore subject to speculation that, in the final analysis, will lead to sudden runs on currency, as shown by the recent history of the capital flows of Argentina, Venezuela, and Mexico, for example. As is known, such movements do not result necessarily from irrational behavior by speculators but, on the contrary, are perfectly predictable and understandable if the inconsistency in domestic economic policies is flagrant and frequent.

Concluding Remarks

Brazil's return to the high growth levels of the 1970s — around 8.5 percent per year — basically depends on the strength of its domestic savings and a better use of foreign savings. In the 1970s, average total savings amounted to 23 percent of the GDP (7 percent corresponded in public savings, 12.2 percent in private savings, and only 3.5 percent in foreign savings). Thus, in light of the precarious nature of public accounts, it is apparent that Brazil aggressively must seek out foreign financing if the economy is to grow at a rate greater than the current yearly rate of 3 to 4 percent.

The rise of new instruments for obtaining foreign funding makes it possible to increase the extent to which Brazil taps foreign savings, even to a level greater than that of the 1970s. Even so, the concern that naturally arises is that the country will become too dependent on foreign capital, mainly the short-term variety. This type of situation would increase the vulnerability of Brazil's balance of payments to speculative movements characteristic of a global economy. In this sense, the stabilization efforts underway become extremely important to the extent that they reduce the degree of risk attributed to investing in Brazil, thereby enhancing the medium- and long-term faith of investors in the country.

Although foreign funding has increased considerably in recent years, it is still quite small in relation to the GDP. The degree of economic and political instability still persisting in Brazil, among other factors, is partially responsible for the low levels of foreign funding in relation to GDP. The trend, though, is a decrease in the speculative and volatile nature of foreign investment and an increase in the extent to which such investment contributes to the country's economic development as economic stability becomes a concrete reality.

In fact, there are two factors that need to work side by side to succeed in the effort for a better performance of the Brazilian economy. The stabilization program headed by the government needs to adopt a more realistic exchange rate policy in the sense that a persistently appreciated Real undoubtedly will have severe negative effects on Brazilian exports and will create a trade imbalance that will accumulate month after month generating negative expectations and, eventually, a foreign exchange crisis that risks getting out of control. Dealing with the exchange rate problem basically through low GNP growth rate to avoid imports means underestimating how serious and hard macroeconomic conditions may become in the future.

Conversely, Brazilian companies are developing meaningful skills for competition in a more open economy and a global supply and demand system. Brazilian companies are becoming increasingly more in line with international standards in order to qualify themselves to obtain foreign funding through the mechanisms detailed earlier in this study. This adaptive process is part of the worldwide trend toward economic globalization — a trend in which Brazil finally is playing an increasingly visible role.

Legislation should be altered, and regulations should be fine-tuned so that Brazil can keep pace with this process and can implement new mechanisms for foreign capital and perfect existing mechanisms. It is important that the economic policies adopted during the Brazilian economic stabilization process do not create barriers to foreign funding that would inhibit the formation of foreign savings and thus hamper Brazil on its road to growing once again.

Notes

1.   Defined by the Brazilian Statistics Bureau (IBGE) as the value of durable goods incorporated by domestic production units for use in their production process for a period of not less than one year, as well as the value of goods and services incorporated to fixed capital goods and intended to increase their usable lifespan, yield or production capacity, and the values of services related to installation of such goods.

2.   The method employed by the IBGE in this calculation converts all information relating to inventories to a common price, making the adjustments required and thus obtaining a homogeneous total. This permits estimation of the difference between opening and final inventory balances of each piece of merchandise.

3.   Current revenues consist of direct and indirect taxes, plus other current revenues.

4.   Current expenses are comprised of government expenditures plus subsidies and transfers.

5.   Its value is equivalent to the surplus in Current Transactions with the Rest of the World, changing the sign.

6.   Total gross capital formation over GDP.

7.   Source: Carneiro & Werneck 1992. The method for calculating the domestic savings rate for this figure uses real interest rates charged on foreign and domestic debt.

8.   See Werneck 1986a.

9.   See Carneiro and Modiano 1992.

10. Carneiro and Modiano 1992.

11. Unfortunately, a complete series of data is not available for the period between 1970 and 1979, although the same pattern as described is confirmed for the spare data available.

12. All amounts as percentages of GDP.

13. Law 6404 of December 15, 1976.

14. Brazilian Treasury Fiscal Note.

15. Parent, subsidiary, associated or affiliated companies, or sharing the same parent company.

16. See Banco Nacional de Desenvolvimento Econômico e Social (BNDES) 1994, Bankers Trust Company 1995, and Fortuna 1994.

17. The U.S. Securities & Exchange Commission (the equivalent Brazilian regulatory agency is called the CVM).

18. See Banco Central do Brasil 1994-1995.

19. MERCOSUR is the Southern Cone Common Market, consisting of Argentina, Brazil, Paraguay, and Uruguay.

20. Table 12 only shows the amount of debt owed during the years 1990-1994; it does not show the levels of funding obtained during these years. Although a complete series of data was not available, the figures available on loans paid back each year and funding in loans versus investments allow us to use foreign debt as a proxy.

References

Associação Nacional das Instituições de Mercado Aberto (ANDIMA). 1994a. *Súmula 6: Fundos de Capital Estrangeiro.* Rio de Janeiro: ANDIMA, September.

Associação Nacional das Instituições de Mercado Aberto (ANDIMA). 1994b. *Súmula 11: Debêntures.* Rio de Janeiro: ANDIMA, October.

Associação Nacional das Instituições de Mercado Aberto (ANDIMA). 1994c. *Súmula 15: Nota Promissória.* Rio de Janeiro: ANDIMA, September.

Associação Nacional das Instituições de Mercado Aberto (ANDIMA). 1994d. *Súmula 19: Lançamento de Títulos no Exterior.* Rio de Janeiro: ANDIMA, August.

Associação Nacional das Instituições de Mercado Aberto (ANDIMA). 1994e. *Súmula 20: Fundos Mútuos de Ações.* Rio de Janeiro: ANDIMA, September.

Banco Central do Brasil. 1994. *Boletim,* Volume 30 - nº 7, July.

Banco Central do Brasil. 1995. *Boletim,* Volume 31 - nº 12, December.

Banco Central do Brasil. 1996a. *Boletim,* Volume 32 - nº 1, January and nº 2, February.

Banco Central do Brasil. 1996b. *Divisão de Suprimentos,* January.

Banco Central do Brasil. 1994-1995. *Análise do Mercado de Câmbio,* 3 rd quarter, 1994 and 1st quarter, 1995.

Barros, Otavio, and Ana Paula F. Mendes. 1994. "O Financiamento Externo Brasileiro e a Captação de Recursos via Títulos e Bônus." *Revista do BNDES.* Rio de Janeiro: BNDES, June.

Banco Nacional de Desenvolvimento Econômico e Social (BNDES). 1994. *Relatório Mercado Internacional.* GEROM/DECAP. Rio de Janeiro: BNDES, July.

Bankers Trust Company-Corporate Trust and Agency Group. 1995. *American Depository Receipts Handbook.* New York: Bankers Trust Co.

Carneiro, Dionísio D., and Rogério L.F. Werneck. 1992. "Public Savings and Private Investment: Requirements for Growth Resumption in the Brazilian Economy." Text for Discussion nº 283. Economics Dept., PUC-RJ. Rio de Janeiro: PUC-RJ.

Carneiro, Dionísio, and Eduardo Modiano. 1992. "Ajuste Externo e Desequilíbrio Interno: 1980-1984." *A Ordem do Progresso - Cem Anos de Política Econômica Republicana.* Rio de Janeiro: Ed. Campus.

Carneiro, Dionísio, Rogério L. F. Werneck, Marcio Garcia, and Miguel A. Bonomo. 1994. "El Fortalecimiento del Sector Financiero en la Economia Brasileña." In *El Fortalecimiento del Sector Financiero en el Proceso de Ajuste: Liberalizacion y Regulacion,* ed. Roberto Frenkel. Buenos Aires: CEDES.

Coopers & Lybrand. 1995. *The Financial Jungle - A Guide to Financial Investment,* eds. Phil Rivett and Peter Speak. New York: Coopers & Lybrand.

Comissão de Valores Mobiliários (CVM). 1994. *Superintendência de Relações com Empresas - Registro e Cancelamento de Companhias Abertas e Sociedades Incentivadas.* Rio de Janeiro: CVM, September.

Fortuna, Eduardo. 1994. *Mercado Financeiro: Produtos e Serviços*, 4th edition. Rio de Janeiro: Qualitymark Editora.

Frenkel, Roberto. 1994. *El Fortalecimento del Sector Financiero en el Proceso de Ajuste: Liberalizacion y Regulacion.* Buenos Aires: CEDES.

Garcia, Marcio G. P. 1994. *Foreign Investment: Regulatory Framework.* Economics Dept. PUC- RJ. Rio de Janeiro: PUC-RJ.

Rosseti, José P. 1988. *Contabilidade Social*, 4th edition. São Paulo: Ed. Atlas.

Sá, Geraldo T. 1994. *Captação de Recursos: Uma Ampla Abordagem - Abordagem Nacional.* Rio de Janeiro: ANDIMA.

Werneck, Rogério L. F. 1986a. "Government Savings, Foreign Debt and Public Sector Financial Crisis." Text for Discussion n" 121, Economics Dept. PUC-RJ. Rio de Janeiro: PUC-RJ.

Werneck, Rogério L. F. 1986b. "Retomada do Crescimento e Esforço de Poupança: Limitações e Possibilidades." Texto para Discussão nº 133, Dept. de Economia da PUC-RJ. Rio de Janeiro: PUC-RJ.

Zagury, Isaac R. 1993. *Captação de Recursos: Uma Ampla Abordagem - Abordagem Internacional.* Rio de Janeiro: ANDIMA.

Chapter 4

The Use of ADRs to Finance Investment in Colombia and Latin America

Roberto Curci
Fernando Jaramillo

Introduction

This study examines the use of American Depository Receipts (ADRs) as instruments for financing investment in Latin America, particularly in Colombia. ADRs historically were issued mostly on behalf of industrial country borrowers. During the 1990s, these instruments have been used by Latin American commercial and industrial firms, financial institutions, and governments to obtain external savings for investment in the development of the region.

Until recently, a major obstacle to the growth of financing for Latin American development has been the slow evolution of domestic capital markets. This slow progress reflects the low volume of local savings in the region. In a sense, the problem is circular: Savings can only be increased by an intensification of productive activity, a condition which, in turn, requires an abundance of savings. It is the role of capital markets, as vehicles for converting savings into investment, to help break this vicious circle. Capital markets should channel domestic and foreign savings toward industrial and commercial activities and promote such activity when there is insufficient supply of investment resources.

The modest size of local capital markets is a main reason why Latin American governments and firms must seek external savings to finance modernization and industrial restructuring. In Colombia the national financial sector is still very small, and trading in stock shares is relatively limited in comparison with trading other types of securities (such as government bonds and bank deposits). Furthermore, in addition to low levels of domestic savings, differentials in domestic and international interest rates provide further incentives for using external savings, whose cost (even after expected devaluation of the peso) is lower.

In Colombia the sale of stock shares via ADRs was made possible by Law 27 of 1990. This law permits firms to issue equity shares paying preferred dividends without voting rights. It should be stressed that the ADRs can be used to represent other types of securities (see Appendix).

In Colombia there is little awareness of the use of ADRs. The clearest expression of this unfamiliarity is the lack of any guides for orienting the public who might be interested in ADRs. Thus, this chapter begins by defining the theoretical and legal frameworks of ADRs and then discusses the present situation and outlook for ADRs, as well as trends for the future. Conclusions regarding the use of these securities are presented at the end of the chapter, along with a glossary of terms so that readers unfamiliar with this topic may understand the terms associated with ADR operations.

Throughout this chapter, "purchasers" refers to financial investors who buy ADR securities, and similarly, "issuers" refers to firms that issue ADRs.

Although there is still limited experience with using ADRs to obtain foreign savings in Latin America, the great majority of cases have been successful. In the future, this strategy of international offerings probably will become more widespread and eventually become a common means of financing for medium- and large-sized Latin American firms.

Institutional Framework

American Depository Receipts (ADRs) are negotiable receipts of deposit that represent one or more depository shares; depository shares, in turn, represent securities issued by a non-American issuer that have been deposited in a custodian bank in the country of origin. ADRs were developed in the United States in 1927 to facilitate U.S. investment in the equity of foreign corporations. Even though ADRs generally represent stock shares, they also may represent other types of securities, such as cumulative preferred shares, bonds, public debt, warrants, or preferred stock.

Depository Shares (DSs) — deposits of securities — are a representation of shares of equity issued by a non-American entity. When the value of an issuer's shares is very low in comparison to stocks traded in the United States, a number of shares must be reissued as a single unit to attain a comparable value; this certificate then constitutes an equivalent value. In the same manner, if the value of the stock is very high, the stock must be split up and the subsequent fraction expressed by a Depository Share.

An ADR is equivalent to one or more Depository Shares, which represent shares of equity in a non-American issuing firm. ADRs are issued for sale to American investors and are negotiable in the United States. To be traded in the rest of the world, similar instruments are floated — Global Depository Receipts, GDRs. GDRs occasionally are alluded to in this study. In such instances, the issue will be referred to as a Global offering.

An ADR represents equity shares of a non-American issuer, that is, a national of a country other than the United States. The ADR program, therefore, allows the issuing firm to place an offering in the United States without being a U.S. entity. ADRs thus facilitate foreign investment in non-

U.S. corporations. At the same time, ADRs reduce trading costs and taxes associated with transfers or exchange regulations, since, as will be shown below, transfers are effected by an intermediary transfer agent.

This intermediary may be a custodian bank in the country of origin of the issue. The custodian bank receives dividends in the local currency and transfers them to the United States in dollars. Similarly, the custodian bank transfers the funds obtained from a flotation in the currency of the country of origin to the issuing firm. These trades also are free from many of the additional formalities that a U.S. citizen faces when buying securities in any of the many marketplaces available for such transactions, such as over-the-counter (OTC) stock exchanges, or through a broker-dealer. In recent years, new applications have been found for ADRs: They have been used to finance foreign mergers, acquisitions, and restructuring of governments' debts.

ADRs can be traded in a number of arenas. These different trading places reflect different types of ADRs. The categories of ADRs and the levels of trading are non-sponsored ADR programs, sponsored ADR programs, level I, level II, level III, and private sales. Each of these programs will now be analyzed.

Non-sponsored ADR Programs

Non-sponsored ADRs are issued by one or more depository banks in response to market demand. They are offered without any formal agreement between the bank and the issuing company, which is located outside the United States. Generally, this type of ADR is offered in response to the interest of investors, broker-dealers, and the depository bank. Most often the depository bank is the principal originator of non-sponsored ADR programs, and the bank seeks to satisfy American investor interest in a specific stock issued by a non-U.S. company.

These programs normally are run by the investors interested in holding ADRs and who contract with a depository bank to issue such receipts. The bank, in turn, contracts with a custodian bank and transfer agent in the country where the securities originate. These originating-country institutions receive the shares and dividends from the corporation whose shares are being traded and transfer them to the depository bank in the United States. The distribution of information to shareholders is another service that can be contracted. At this level of ADR transaction, the depository bank is not obligated to name a proxy to vote for the ADR holders.

Thus, non-sponsored ADR programs proceed without being floated by the corporation issuing the equity. This means that the originating company whose shares are being held and reissued as ADRs does not raise new funds through this mechanism, but rather it allows U.S. investors to buy the derivative ADRs (and build up demand for its shares).

The depository bank usually requests a letter of no-objection to the issue of ADRs from the issuing corporation, but this consent is not compulsory. Nevertheless, the U.S. Securities and Exchange Commission's (SEC) registration requirements often call for information that the depository bank cannot supply directly. Thus, in many instances, ADR programs may be developed only if the corporation whose shares are to be held on deposit cooperates and supplies the necessary information.

In some cases, the fees associated with issuing ADRs may be reduced if two or more banks issue receipts of deposit for the same class of shares from a single corporation.

Sponsored ADR Programs

Sponsored ADRs are issued by a depository bank in the United States at the request of a foreign corporation. This relationship takes the form of either a deposit or a service contract.

Sponsored ADRs differ from unsponsored programs in that the rights and obligations of the foreign corporation are established formally in the deposit agreement subscribed with the depository bank. Furthermore, the issuing corporation signs Form 6, the report submitted to the SEC to register the shares in the United States.

Another difference is that the depository bank is required to inform the ADR holders in a timely fashion of any information that may be of interest to them. The holders of sponsored ADRs also may exercise their voting rights through the bank, which names a representative to serve in the country of origin of the equity. This representative also consults with the depository bank regarding decisions to be taken at stockholders' meetings.

Sponsorship does not imply any reporting other than what is required by the SEC for registration. The final way in which sponsored ADRs differ from non-sponsored ADRs is that, in the case of the former, administrative costs, fees, and expenses related to the stockholder, as well as postage, are not distributed by agreement among the depository bank and the holders of the ADRs. In the case of sponsored ADRs, the issuing firm assumes all the costs of the primary operation since the secondary costs are the responsibility of the receipt holders. The secondary costs include, for example, paying off the shares, the division of ADRs, endorsements, and so on.

Level I (Sponsored or Non-sponsored)

The Level I ADR programs are the simplest since they involve few requisites and are traded in the OTC market. Level I ADRs are among the fastest-growing categories. They represent between 5 and 15 percent of the total shares of the corporations that issue them. Among these corporations are such well-known firms as Nintendo, Rolls-Royce, Banesto, and Volkswagen. At this level, sponsored or non-sponsored ADRs can be traded.

In this case, the shares — or any other type of security traded on the secondary market in the country of origin — are deposited in the custodian bank for the purpose of issuing ADRs in the United States by the depository bank, which has the contract with the custodian bank to execute this function, as well as with a transfer agent (which may be the custodian bank itself). Trading in specific ADRs is created by the OTC market makers.

It is important to stress that Level I ADRs are not sold as part of a public offering. Thus, they are exempt from registration statements to the SEC under the provisions of the Securities Act of 1933. Nor are Level I ADRs listed on the New York Stock Exchange (NYSE), the American Stock Exchange (AMEX), or the National Association of Securities Dealers Automated Quotation System (NASDAQ). In other words, transactions at this level are private.

Since this class of ADRs is traded in the OTC market, issuers of such equities must satisfy a minimum of requirements to trade. For the issuing corporation, Level I ADRs provide access to a large group of investors with few transaction costs. Although Level I ADRs are not listed on any national market, this type of ADR reaches North American investors, and the typical markets are the pink sheet listings of over-the-counter securities and the specialized bulletins, such as the Bulletin Board Service.

Corporations based in countries all over the world sell securities at this level: Thailand, Australia, England, Bermuda, Spain, France, Holland, Israel, Singapore, Greece. Within Latin America, firms from Venezuela and Mexico have issued Level I ADRs. Note that at Level I the trade occurs between a consumer and an issuer when the ADR is sponsored in a private market. The issuer uses his/her own market instruments to inform potential clients of the product, and eventually customers formalize their purchases with a broker-dealer specified by the issuer. Nevertheless, the terms of the trade are set between the parties when they communicate.

In this case, a group of investors sets a price for a specific number of shares, and the issuer decides whether this price is acceptable or not. If the issuing corporation finds the transaction reasonable, it sells the shares/ADRs to these already established purchasers, and the sale is finalized by an office designated for this purpose.

Thus, this scenario corresponds to situations in which a preexisting group of investors, after analyzing the strengths of the issuer, decides to purchase the specific ADR, given their expected profit margin or interest in the particular deal.

At Level I, it is common to find the large investor who seeks to acquire a substantial share in a corporation, as well as investors who are invited to participate in the floating of an ADR because they, in conjunction with other investors, may determine the success of an issue and a reasonable price for the issuer.

In Colombia, an individual or a corporation might be interested in becoming an active partner or increasing an investment in a Colombian firm. This may be to further its horizontal growth or to move upstream or downstream in the value chain or just to pursue a large investment.

Such a potential investor would seek information on performance of other firms in the sector of interest and data on the larger economic environment of the firms. Such indicators are available through specialized economic publications. These publications usually also indicate which are the fastest-growing and most promising firms. The financial position of representative firms is also available in broadly circulated magazines and newspapers. In Colombia, for example, this information is found in the publications of the stock exchange and *Money* magazine.

In addition, once having developed a general overview, the potential investor may consult advisors to identify those firms that might be interested in developing financial products as part of their corporate operations. If after contact between the investor (the purchaser) and the issuer there is clear interest between both parties, then up-to-date and accurate information is likely to be presented with any proposal so that the purchaser may make a reasonable decision.

At this level of transaction (Level I), the investor is often a frequent client for other financial products and, as such, is invited to participate in offerings by the issuer. In such instances, the issuer is likely to present a comprehensive overview of the firm's position and set out the advantages of participation in the program offered. Informational pamphlets, prospectuses, and offering circulars are usually available. It is standard practice to hold presentations for brokers and other individuals in a position to influence potential buyers in order to provide them with information to motivate and guide their clients.

Level I ADRs may be a good first step for those corporations that want to test the market, see how they fare, and if advisable, then transact at a higher level. It is important to note that although the prerequisites for trading at Level I are minimal, they do take time to complete. The general requirements are registration by the originating non-U.S. firm with the SEC using Forms F-6 (Securities Act of 1933) and 12G3-2(B) (Securities Exchange Act of 1934).

Level II (Sponsored)

ADRs traded at Level II, in contrast to those at Level I, are listed on the major stock exchanges — the NYSE, AMEX, or NASDAQ — but are not registered public offerings; that is, they continue to be private offerings. However, Level II ADRs must be sponsored. As with Level I issues, securities are deposited with a custodian bank for the purpose of issuing ADRs in the United States by a depository bank that has been contracted to perform this function. In addition, the foreign issuing corporation for Level II ADRs must present a financial and accounting statement prepared in accordance with generally accepted accounting principles (GAAP) and satisfy any other requirements of the specific market in which the securities will be traded. Furthermore, all SEC requirements must be met, and the corporation must assume the continuing costs of reporting.

The advantages of Level II transactions include the considerable publicity and liquidity of operations in these markets. Firms from Australia, England, Italy, Spain, France, Japan, Israel, and Sweden trade at Level II. The majority of these corporations first enter the market at Level I and later go on to Level II or III.

In 1993 the market for this type of securities grew by 20 percent, rising from 215 to 256 programs. The volume in U.S. dollars was around $201 billion, and operations at this level tend to be for amounts ranging between $200 and $700 million.

For Level II transactions, the issuing corporation contracts with an underwriter, who in turn contacts clients and informs them of the features of the product. Since the potential investors tend to be the underwriter's own clients, the underwriter will always first assure the quality of the product in order to satisfy clients. Moreover, the underwriter may use its own informational facilities to inform other potential clients that the firm is recommending the ADR and has it available.

Once potential customers have made the decision to buy, they approach the underwriter with an indication of interest, and a binding commitment to buy is worked out. The commitment is quantified (as to price and number of ADRs) and compared with the quantity of ADRs on sale. If the break-even point is acceptable to the issuer, then the trade is made.

It is important to understand that the underwriter does not necessarily promote a single product exclusively. In most instances, the issuer's ADRs are part of a portfolio of products, and the sponsor's marketing efforts are spread over a broad showcase of products.

Specialized firms that participate in sponsoring these programs, such as the NYSE and AMEX, have their own publications that are read by potential investors. The editors of these publications often recommend specific programs. Given the repute and confidence associated with these advisors, these publications tend to inform and influence buyers' decisions.

The general requirements for trading at Level II are registration of the non-U.S. issuer with the SEC using Form F-6 (Securities Act of 1933) and filing Forms 20-F and 6-K (Securities Exchange Act of 1934).

Level III (Sponsored)

Sponsored Level III ADRs are traded by public offering. The ADRs are listed and registered in compliance with the rules for Levels I and II. In addition, ADRs traded at Level III must satisfy the provisions of the Securities Act of 1933 regarding public offerings. Level III ADRs are issued as receipts for shares transacted in the primary market in the country of the issuing corporation and are backed by new shares. These securities are held on deposit in a custodian bank, so that ADRs may be sold in the United States by the depository bank. The greatest levels of publicity and liquidity are obtained in this market, but all SEC requirements must be fulfilled, and the costs of continuously supplying information must be borne.

Level III ADRs are transacted on the NYSE, AMEX, and NASDAQ. Among the corporations that have traded using this instrument are Hong Kong Telecom, Repsol, Rhone Poulenc, Elf Aquitaine, and the Chilean Telephone Company, CTC. Transactions at this level are realized in amounts ranging between $500,000 and $1 billion.

At this level, there is no personal contact between potential customers and the issuer. Purchasers are likely to decide to acquire the issuer's product from among a large variety of alternatives. Usually, such buyers do not have the capacity for extensive analysis, since the product is only one among many in a large showcase containing many competing products, and the decision to buy is likely to be influenced by the advice of the retail vendor, their broker.

At this level (Sponsored, Level III ADRs), both the issuer and the product must satisfy all legal requirements of the U.S. market, since these products utilize the full range of distribution mechanisms available in the market. This broad exposure implies that the ADRs are available to a great number of small-volume customers, who are protected by the legal regulations.

Level III customers buy ADRs through their stock brokers, who are the final link in the distribution chain at this level. Therefore, this type of ADR is available to the largest number of buyers. These investors usually are advised by their brokers, who in turn obtain information either through knowledge of the issuer or through the product presentations mentioned above in the discussion of trading at Level I. The exchanges themselves also generate information of interest to potential investors.

As mentioned, ADRs traded at Level III must fulfill all requirements for sale on the stock exchanges. The general requisites are registration of the non-U.S. issuer with the SEC using Form F-6 (Securities Act of 1933) and filing of Forms 20-F and 6-K (Securities Exchange Act of 1934).

Private Placements

In this case, the ADRs are sold privately among large institutional investors — Qualified Institutional Buyers (QIBs) — under provisions of SEC Rule 144A of the Securities Act of 1933. These transactions are executed via Private Offerings, Resales, and Trading through Automated Linkages (PORTAL).

There are many benefits accompanying the sale of ADRs through private placements. First, private placements attract a large number of QIBs, since very few QIBs are experienced in foreign investment and SEC regulations also prohibit many of them from investing in non-dollar-denominated securities. Second, private placements also involve additional registration rights, such as piggyback rights, in the event that the issuer later opts for a public offering or lists the securities on a national market. Third, the costs are lower in private sales since no global custodian is needed. Furthermore, after two or three years of restriction, these securities may be traded without having to be registered with the SEC or combined with a sponsored Level I program (OTC).

Private placements are the most expeditious mechanism for any corporation wishing to sell its securities in the U.S. market. Even though all SEC requirements must be satisfied, securities may be traded among QIBs through international underwriters. This mechanism allows for faster sales than transactions among non-qualified investors. Furthermore, the placement is more likely to be successful than in other markets, given the financial strength of the investors who routinely trade large blocks of shares. Thus, private placement of ADRs is a very attractive alternative when there are sufficient conditions for a private offering.

The Legal Framework of ADRs

Issuers of ADRs should be aware of two major aspects of U.S. securities legislation. First, under the Securities Act of 1933, ADRs and the equity shares on deposit are considered as independent securities — though, in practice, the ADRs merely represent the shares on deposit. Public offering of ADRs in the United States (Level III) requires registration with the SEC of both the ADRs and the securities on deposit. In the case of Levels I and II, ADRs are registered and issued under the Securities Act of 1933. However, if the foreign issuing corporation is not sponsoring the offering, only the ADRs have to be registered with the SEC. In this case, the equity shares on deposit are exempt from registration. For example, when an investor buys a security in a secondary market in a foreign country and leaves it on deposit in a depository or custodian bank, this type of share is exempt from registration. Nevertheless, ADRs issued with the backing of a depository bank must be registered if they do not qualify for any other exemption. Finally, an issuer that has registered its equities must file a report every year with the SEC. These reports are filed by submitting Forms SEC 20-F and 6-K, which are basically annual financial reports.

The second aspect of U.S. securities legislation that applies importantly to ADR issuers appears in the Securities and Exchange Act of 1934. Foreign corporations issuing ADRs for trade in the OTC market at Level I under Rule 12G3-2(B) of the Act may request exemption from registration. Nevertheless, an issuing corporation whose securities on deposit are registered under the Securities Act of 1933, and whose ADRs are listed on a U.S. exchange or on the NASDAQ, also must register the securities on deposit under the 1934 Act. As a result, the corporation also must file annual reports with the SEC using Form 20-F and periodic reports using Form 6-K.

Once the initial requirements have been fulfilled, potential customers are given an offering prospectus for their consideration. This prospectus does not have to contain an offer price nor other important information, such as the underwriter's name or the date of the issue. Such information may be included if desired. The offering prospectus must be registered with the SEC.

It is important to stress that ADRs are programs that represent offerings made outside the United States. Thus, these transactions also are regulated by the authorities that supervise securities exchange in the specific country of issue. In Colombia, public sale of preferred stock is regulated and overseen by the Superintendent of Securities (Superintendencia de Valores).

An offering may be split into three parts: one in Colombia, the second in the United States, and the third in the rest of the world. The first part of the offering would be a traditional placement of securities on the local market; the second part would involve ADRs, and the third part would involve GDRs.

In any event, to issue ADRs for shares on deposit, Form F-6 must be filed with the SEC, under the Exchange Act of 1933, unless an exemption is applicable. The SEC, which adopted Form F-6 for the registration of ADRs, requires that the three steps below be met in the following order:

1. The depository bank must entitle the holder of ADRs to redeem them or withdraw the securities on deposit on demand, merely by handing over the ADR titles, subject only to certain restrictions.

2. The securities on deposit, if sold in the United States, must be offered or sold in transactions registered under the provisions of the Securities Act of 1933 or in transactions exempt from registration.

3. Upon registration through SEC Form F-6, the corporation issuing the securities on deposit must conform with the 1934 Act reporting requirements or else be exempt from reporting under the provisions of SEC Rule 12G3-2(B).

The situation is different when the foreign firm is trading in the over-the-counter market (Level I). In this case, the issuer may request exemption from registration under the 1933 Act and instead register under the 1934 Act, without having to register under both.

At some point, an issuer may decide that its Level I ADRs should be traded as listed ADRs in the secondary market at Level II. This decision might be associated with objectives of reaching a broader market of investors, further promoting the ADRs, and maybe even reaching Level III, the category in which ADRs are transacted in a public offering.

To enter the primary and secondary markets of the stock exchange, ADRs must be listed on the NYSE, the AMEX, or the NASDAQ. To be listed on the NYSE or the AMEX, an ADR must be sponsored. The NASDAQ further requires that ADRs be registered simultaneously under the 1933 and 1934 Acts. In other words, the ADRs must be traded in a registered public offering. If trading on the NASDAQ, the issuer also must present periodic reports to the SEC.

When listing on the NYSE (or the AMEX), the issuing company may qualify to be listed on the standard domestic list or on a standard alternate list for non-U.S. issuing firms. This decision is left to the issuer. The standard domestic list is made up of securities issued by both U.S. corporations and foreign firms, while the alternate standard list consists of securities issued by foreign companies. Issuing corporations are responsible for all fees. Presently, these fees include a basic initial charge of $36,800 and additional pro-rated fees adjusted to the size of the issue: $14,750 for the first and second million dollars, $7,400 for the third and fourth million dollars, $3,500 per million from the fifth to the 300th million dollars, after which the fee is $1,900 per million. In any event, the minimum charge is $100,000, and there are additional annual fees that must be paid to remain listed.

To qualify for the standard domestic list, the foreign issuer must have at least 2,000 stockholders in the United States, who each hold 100 or more shares, or at least 2,200 U.S. shareholders and an average volume of 100,000 shares. Also, at least 1,100,000 shares must be in circulation in the United States, and their total market value must exceed $18 million. The net worth of the issuing corporation must be greater than or equal to $18 million, and 1) its net income before taxes must be at least $2.5 million in the most recent fiscal year and $2 million during each of the prior two years, or 2) the cumulative income over the three prior years must total at least $6.5 million, with profits in each year, and an income of at least $4.5 million during the most recent year. Obviously, these requirements limit the Latin American firms' access to the standard list.

ADRs traded at Level III must be listed on the alternate standard list. To qualify for this mode of trading on the NYSE or the AMEX, the issuing firm must satisfy the following conditions: possess at least 5,000 stockholders worldwide, each of whom holds 100 or more shares; have at least 2.5 million shares in circulation whose total market value is greater than $100 million; have a net worth of at least $100 million; and have cumulative pre-tax earnings over the three preceding years of at least $100 million and minimum annual earnings before taxes of at least $25 million for each of the three preceding years.

In December 1993, the Colombian Superintendencia de Valores passed Resolution 1447. This new regulation modified the system of public offerings in order to modernize operations and intensify their use. Market value pricing was adopted for Colombian securities, thereby pricing shares in the same manner as ADRs that are offered in the United States. Through this legislation, Colombia began to adjust to international market trends so that national firms could gain experience with such instruments and overcome their reluctance to appear on world markets.

In a January 23, 1994, article in the newspaper *El Tiempo*, analysts from the brokerage house Corredores Asociados maintained that this resolution was a source of new obstacles since it established a series of requirements for simultaneous public offerings in the local and international markets: Only firms with a high rating of creditworthiness for the previous year could offer publicly stocks or bonds redeemable in stocks. Nevertheless, corporations whose securities were registered on the stock exchange during the year prior to the offering could proceed if they offered shares on the Colombian market at least three months prior to their international sale.

According to the article cited, for all practical purposes, the resolution made it impossible for new corporations or firms with a medium level of creditworthiness to issue ADRs or GDRs. The requirement of a high creditworthiness rating is a barrier for many firms. On the other hand, if the firm persists in trying to go out into the international market, it will face problems related to setting an offering price for the issue. It is very likely that if the base price is considered "low," the local demand for securities during the prior three-month period will be so high that all the shares will be sold and it will be impossible to make an international offering. Yet if the price is considered "high," the local demand will be so low that a foreign investor will not be likely to find attractive securities that could not be sold in Colombia. If this happens, it also will be impossible to access international markets. This paradoxical situation was unresolved at the end of 1995.

Financing Mechanisms with ADRs
Present Situation and Trends

For some time now, there has been an ongoing boom in foreign securities in U.S. markets. Most U.S. investors hope to spread their portfolio risk by investing in high yield securities. According to a survey of investors by Broadgate Consultants, Inc., 84 percent of the respondents hoped to increase their investments in such securities. Only 15 percent wanted to remain at their current level of investments. Given that the surveyed investors control over US$3 billion in securities, even a slight change in the ratios invested implies tremendous volatility in foreign stock exchanges, especially those located in emerging economies.

According to a report on the depository receipt market issued by The Bank of New York — *The 1993 Depository Receipt Market Review* — in 1992, non-U.S. firms captured $9.4 billion in financial resources through the sale of ADRs, a 36 percent increase over the previous year. U.S. stock exchanges, such as the NYSE, the AMEX, and the NASDAQ, realized nearly $125 billion in ADR transactions. Mexican firms realized 11 offerings, followed by eight issues by English corporations, and four by Australian firms. Several of these offerings, by firms such as Telefonos de Mexico and Welcome PLC, attracted as much as $1 billion. Overall, 112 new offerings took place. The issuing corporations were from over 40 countries. Although Mexico presently has issued the greatest number of Latin American ADRs, Chile was the first country to venture into the U.S. market. Now firms from countries such as Venezuela, Argentina, Brazil, and, more recently, Colombia are competing internationally to attract financial resources.

The ADR market in 1993 reached record levels for volume of trade, for funds raised, and for the number of ADR programs launched. There were 124 publicly traded programs, a 32 percent increase over the 85 programs launched in 1992. These sponsored ADR programs were issued by corporations from 28 different countries; 6.3 billion ADRs were traded, and these transactions raised $200 billion. The volume of ADRs transacted rose 46.5 percent, and the amount captured was 60 percent more than in 1992. These data only reflect transactions on stock exchanges (the NYSE, the AMEX, and the NASDAQ). They do not include ADRs traded on the secondary markets. Corporations from Great Britain, Mexico, and Holland were the most active in 1993. There was also strong activity among firms from South Africa, France, Argentina, and Hong Kong with considerable trade volume. Since 1990, the number of ADRs traded has increased by over 65 percent, while the growth in dollars has doubled. The continued performance of ADR programs has demonstrated that large investors prefer to invest through ADR programs when they invest in securities of foreign firms.

During 1993, with 50 offerings in U.S. public markets, non-U.S. firms attracted approximately $10 billion, almost double the $5.3 billion traded the year before. Nearly one-half of these securities were sold by Latin American corporations — almost all of which were Mexican or Argentine firms. The remaining securities were sold by European firms. In July 1993, one of the largest ADR offerings was carried out by the Argentine government when it privatized Yacimientos Petrolíferos Fiscales S.A., the state oil company. With ADRs listed on the NYSE, the government tapped $2.38 billion. In 1993, under the provisions of Rule 144A, 33 private placements took place. These ADR offerings attracted over $2 billion. Of the total capital attained under Rule 144A, approximately 40 percent was obtained by Asian firms, 30 percent by Latin American firms, and 30 percent by European corporations.

Of the developed regions, Europe remained the most attractive area for investors. Also, Canada and Australia maintain a large share of the market. However, the emerging economies are enjoying very high growth rates thanks to efforts made by local stock exchanges in recent years.

The economic conditions now prevalent in Latin America have assured investors that perspectives for the economies of Mexico, Brazil, Argentina, Chile, Venezuela, and Colombia are promising and that solid investment opportunities are available in these countries.

Such factors as the opening of domestic economies, the privatization of state firms, the reduction of public spending, improved corporate financial performance, and the deregulation of foreign investment and capital repatriation have had a notable influence on the resurgence of capital markets in the region.

In the past, concern with political instability or underdevelopment in the emerging countries prevented North American investors from seriously considering Latin America as a market for their portfolios. Now the region is seen as a good investment opportunity.

The North American market has demonstrated the fastest growth. According to Intersec Research, this market will grow 25 percent in the coming years. The volume of the U.S. market for 1994 is expected to be $225 billion. This growth largely reflects the poor performance of the Japanese stock market, political problems in the former Soviet Union, and the repercussions of these events in European markets. For these reasons, firms in search of capital and investors have come to see ADRs as a very useful vehicle for implementing development plans, privatizing state firms, or gaining greater international exposure for a particular corporation.

The first Latin American corporation to issue ADRs was the Compañía de Teléfonos de Chile, the Chilean telephone company. In mid-1990, it sold $93 million of ADRs on the NYSE. Since these first trades, many Latin American firms have passed through the U.S. markets.

ADRs and Colombian Borrowers

After Decree 444 was issued in 1967, the Colombian capital markets went into decline. This decline was largely due to a "stream of taxes that burdened firms, the tax rate on corporations, the non-deductibility of interest, and the capital gains taxes that had to be paid with the appreciation of shares on the market."[1]

Approximately 10 years ago, 193 corporations traded securities on the Bogotá stock market.[2] As a result of taxes and strict market regulations, firms lost interest in the stock market and turned to commercial indebtedness, which was much cheaper. The number of corporations trading securities fell until only 83 corporations were trading on the exchange. More recently, there has been a rapid growth in the volume of trade in Colombia. This increased volume may be attributed to a number of factors: economic opening, government promotion of stock markets as low cost sources of financing for firms, new accounting and tax regulations, new and appropriate market technologies, and a more sophisticated finance culture, as well as the entry of new market participants.

Large Colombian financial groups and firms currently perceive international markets as providing opportunities to strengthen their share capital. As a result, an increasing number of private and public institutions have been offering stocks, bonds, and Euronotes. Over the past 12 months, there has been a boom in offerings, especially by firms linked to the larger Colombian financial and business groups.

The standard for international stock operations by Colombian firms was set by the Corporación Financiera del Valle. In 1993, this firm raised $40 million with an issue of preferred stock. This offering was placed internationally using ADRs. A total of six million shares were sold, four million in international markets and two million locally. In the local market, each share sold for 5,000 Colombian pesos; the ADRs, which represented two shares each, sold for $13. The ADR offering raised $27 million. The Corporación Financiera del Valle contracted the services of specialized organizations such as the International Finance Corporation, Merrill Lynch, Bear Stearns, and Baring Brothers. Citibank was the depository bank.

The Corporación Financiera del Valle operation stimulated other financial institutions to carry out similar operations. Thus, in November 1993, Banco Ganadero issued ADRs in the amount of $90 million. These securities were sold especially in U.S. and European markets. For this ADR program, Merrill Lynch served as the international underwriter and Citibank as the depository bank.

Given the success of this first incursion into international markets, Banco Ganadero decided to go further and registered another offering with the SEC on October 27, 1994. This second offering consisted of 7.2 million ADRs — each representing 100 ordinary class B shares — with a nominal value of $10 per share, which were to be sold on the NYSE. With this offering, Banco Ganadero became the first Colombian financial institution to carry out an international operation at this level.

In fact, the international financial community has recognized the performance of Colombian firms, as seen recently when Standard & Poors granted Colombian bonds an investment grade rating. Furthermore, the Colombian financial sector maintained its status as the most attractive area for foreign investors in 1993.

The sale of international securities by Colombian financial institutions has not been restricted to offerings by the Corporación Financiera del Valle and Banco Ganadero. Banco de Colombia also began its incursion into foreign markets with securities such as Euronotes and preferred stock shares packaged as ADRs. The Banco de Colombia's first foreign issuance operation took place in 1993 when, in its official capacity, the bank issued a package of Euronotes.

In April 1994, Cementos Diamante (Diamond Cement) became the first industrial corporation to use ADR-type instruments to raise capital. The firm raised $38 million selling ADRs and $19 million selling GDRs. Baring Brothers, Bear Stearns, and Morgan Grenfell were the institutional advisors for Cementos Diamante, and Citibank International served as the depository bank.

Subsequently, a number of additional Colombian borrowers entered the market. In June 1994, Carulla, a traditional Colombian supermarket chain, offered ADRs and GDRs for a total value of $26 million. Baring Brothers was in charge of the offering for Carulla. In September 1994, another cement firm, Cementos Paz del Rio, raised $62 million by offering ADRs. Finally, in December 1994, another traditional supermarket chain, Cadenalco, issued an offering for approximately $37 million. Of this amount, 65 percent was transacted in Europe and the United States.

Nevertheless, there have been stumbling blocks along the path of trading shares on international markets. Toward the end of the last trimester of 1994, Banco de Colombia — then already in private hands — and Banco Ganadero had to postpone ADR issues for approximately $150 million and $200 million, respectively, because of a rise in U.S. interest rates, which depressed the stock market. Both banks had to put off their offerings until market conditions improved.

Colombian firms continue to be interested in acquiring fresh resources abroad. There is great interest in the operation to be realized by the holding company recently formed by the banker Luis Carlos Sarmiento Angulo. Distrall and Icollantas had offerings ready to be issued among international investors by the end of 1994. Likewise, the financial concerns owned by Luis Carlos Sarmiento's organization, such as the Banco Industrial Colombiano, announced that they would raise capital by issuing shares abroad. As a result of successes up to now, the number of Colombian firms trading ADRs will probably rise in the near future.

Trends

As a financial product, ADRs are relatively new. It was only about 20 years ago that U.S. investors began to deal actively in this product. To date, ADRs have proved to be an important alternative for attracting foreign investment to many countries. The number of ADR programs increases each year, suggesting a growth stage with great prospects in the future. The number of ADR programs over the past eight years follows:

Total ADR Programs	
Year	Number of Programs
1986	700
1987	754
1988	782
1989	804
1990	836
1991	886
1992	924
1993	996

Source: The Bank of New York, *1993 Market Review*.

The high levels of U.S. investment in foreign issues, including investments in mutual funds, made 1993 an unprecedented year. This interest was largely due to purchases of Latin American and Asian issues. That year's performance has helped demand for securities in many world markets. Major buying activity occurred during 1994 because of the continued global trend toward privatization, as well as a shift of overall investing in favor of emerging markets. These trends have stimulated the launching of many ADR programs.

Given the size of the world market and the volume of investments, it is almost impossible to measure the number of firms that could use ADRs to enter international financial markets. In principle, the number of potential competitors for capital acquisition through ADR issuance consists of all those firms throughout the world that could qualify under SEC rules.

The number of ADR programs offered during 1993 rose to 996 from throughout the world. The following table breaks down the structure of the supply of ADR programs by country of origin:

ADR Programs by Country of Issuer	
Country	**Percent of Total Supply**
Great Britain	21.1
Australia	17.5
Japan	14.8
South Africa	8.6
Hong Kong	5.1
Mexico	4.7
France	2.7
Holland	2.6
Germany	2.5
Italy	2.4
Malaysia	1.6
Others	16.4

Source: The Bank of New York, *1993 Market Review.*

The structure of the Latin American supply of ADR programs by country of origin in 1993 was as follows:

ADR Programs by Latin American Issuers	
Country	**Percentage of Total L. Am. ADRs**
Mexico	61
Argentina	11
Chile	11
Brazil	8
Venezuela	8
Others	1

With regard to Colombia, even though the country's domestic market is quite competitive, this market is still sufficiently small that funding at the level of ADR issues (typically, US$100 million or more) is unusual and would have a major impact on the market. This means that ADR financing for a Colombian company will provide a challenge for organizing the large-scale issue, as well as a benefit of escaping the historical barrier to financing at such a scale in the domestic market. To put this in perspective, in 1993 non-U.S. corporations raised $10 billion through 50 ADR programs in public markets (at Level III). By contrast, the estimated total value of ADRs issued by Colombian firms in U.S. markets was about $200 million.

Even though in the global context Colombia's needs are small, the strengths of the Colombian market are very significant. Dozens of firms possess the size and performance quality that would enable them to compete in the ADR issuance market. Within Colombia, however, the idea of utilizing ADRs is relatively new. This is confirmed by the very small number of firms that have issued ADRs to date. There is clearly a need for Colombian firms to familiarize themselves with this and other foreign financing mechanisms.

The relatively limited penetration of Colombian firms in the ADR market also has another facet — namely, the issue of country risk. It is important to recall that ADR prices and marketability depend on two components: the quality of the firm itself and the environment in which the firm operates. Economic, social, and political variables are extremely significant for products such as ADRs, since the rate of return on such investments is determined by two elements: the financial performance of the issuing firm and the performance of the country's currency. As a result, the economic, social, and political setting is included in any financial product analysis by investors concerned with minimizing their risk.

In the case of Colombia, the macroeconomic aspect of ADR issues has been strengthened by ongoing economic stability. Nevertheless, there continues to be some uncertainty regarding social and political affairs. This uncertainty means that the Colombian issuer of ADRs must be in a sufficiently attractive position to attract investors despite this source of perceived risk. This situation also may explain why Colombian ADR issues have been composed of preferred stocks, which guarantee higher dividends than ordinary shares. Even in the worst case, these dividends are never less than those paid on common stock.

The programs launched abroad by Colombian firms until now leave a positive legacy. The rate of growth of gross domestic product (GDP) during 1994-1996 is a favorable indicator for investment, and the free trade agreements with Mexico and Venezuela and with Andean Pact countries establish a range of security and stability. In addition, a number of Latin American firms have marketed their programs successfully, with the number of ADR — and GDR — programs on the rise. These factors suggest a positive medium-term trend for ADR programs issued by Colombian firms. As long as factors beyond the control of firms remain positive in the future, the participation of Colombian ADRs in the market should increase and thereby increase foreign investment in the country.

Conclusion

The benefits of issuing ADRs are multiple, both for the issuing corporations and for investors. These benefits include increasing the market for a firm's shares among a broad and diversified array of investors (which may increase or stabilize a stock's price); broadening and improving the image of a company's products not only in the local market, but also internationally; providing a mechanism with which to increase a firm's capital at relatively low cost; and increasing the market for other securities, such as bonds and preferred stocks. For the investors, ADRs allow for global portfolio diversification without dealing with the costs and risks of participating directly in foreign securities exchanges.

Although investors increasingly are diversifying their investments to reduce risk in their portfolios, foreign business styles, unknown foreign investment policies, additional taxes, and other market idiosyncrasies often discourage institutions from investing in foreign markets. For this reason, ADRs have emerged as a financial instrument that very well suits the needs of U.S. investors. ADRs are tradeable securities, denominated and paying dividends in dollars; they are free of the problems associated with owning securities outside the United States, and, finally, ADRs are highly liquid, both in the U.S. market and in the original market of issue, since they are interchangeable with the home-country shares.

ADR programs are an interesting mechanism through which the Colombian government and firms can raise capital abroad. ADRs simultaneously generate foreign financial resources that add to domestic savings, and they support the process of opening and modernizing the economy.

Appendix

The following comments draw on the tables presented in this Appendix. These tables were prepared by The Bank of New York and published in the *1993 Market Review*.

Globally, ADR programs stimulate important flows of resources, regardless of whether the transactions take the form of private offerings, Rule 144A private placements (Figure 1), or any other categories of transaction. In 1993 the total trade in ADRs represented 5.4 percent of the total transacted on stock exchanges ($3,690 billion, Figure 2). ADRs attracted $9.538 billion (Figure 3). The growth of these programs is evident: In 1986 there were only 700 ADR programs; by 1993 the number had risen to 996. This growth trend has been sustained over the last seven years (Figure 4).

Regarding the types of programs, in 1986 there were only 87 sponsored programs. As firms came to recognize the value of ADRs, the number of sponsored offerings has increased. Thus, by 1993 sponsored offerings had increased to 584, a 6.71-fold increase (Figure 5).

By country, the largest number of programs (Figure 6) and sponsored programs (Figure 7) have been issued by corporations based in Great Britain. This primacy is also reflected in the dollar volume transacted, which is not necessarily proportionate to the quantity of ADR programs launched (Figure 8). Similarly, a large share (26.5 percent) of public offerings (Level II and III ADRs) originate in Great Britain. France, on the other hand, heads the list of private and Rule 144A offerings, with a 21.2 percent share of the capital attracted. In terms of number of programs, France comes in fourth (Figure 9). In this category, Colombia is in next to last place, between Australia and Norway.

The leading depository bank is The Bank of New York. It ranks first in the number of new programs sponsored (60.5 percent, Figure 10), in the number of all programs sponsored (53.8 percent, Figure 11), and in the conversion of non-sponsored ADRs into sponsored programs (78 percent). The other principal depository banks involved in such conversions are Morgan and Citibank. The conversion of non-sponsored programs (Figure 12) reflects corporate interest in establishing ADR programs in an enduring form. The Bank of New York is also the leader in programs listed on the stock exchanges, with a 57 percent share of this category (Figure 13). If the subgroup of ADR programs that are listed and sponsored is examined, The Bank of New York is also at the head, with a 46.4 percent share.

In Colombia there is no defined trend in preferences for international underwriters or depository banks for national offerings, which is probably a reflection of the still low number of programs. There is, however, a clear predominance of the Colombian financial sector in issuing ADRs. This sector accounts for 41 percent of the ADR programs realized, followed in second place by manufacturing. This trend is likely to hold, since almost all the offerings under study for 1995 are connected with the financial sector.

The apparent independence or low correlation between returns on Colombian stock exchanges and exchanges in the rest of Latin America may facilitate an increase in Colombian participation in the ADR market. This independence generates confidence in the country and stimulates the U.S. investor to purchase programs associated with Colombian firms.

Figure 1.
Summary of the Rule 144A Depository Receipts Market

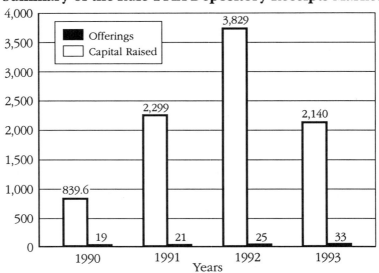

Source: The Bank of New York, Depository Receipts (ADRs and GDRs), *1993 Market Review.*
Note: In 1993 there were 35 private offers of depository receipts, 33 of which fell under Rule 144A.

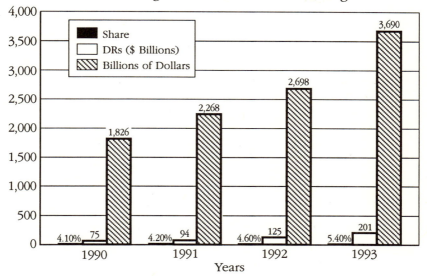

Figure 2.
Volume of Depository Receipts Traded
as a Percentage of all Trade on the Exchanges

Source: The Bank of New York, Depository Receipts (ADRs and GDRs), *1993 Market Review*.

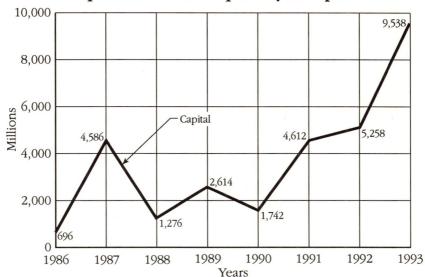

Figure 3.
Capital Raised with Depository Receipts

Source: The Bank of New York, Depository Receipts (ADRs and GDRs), *1993 Market Review*.

Figure 4.
Total Number of ADR Programs

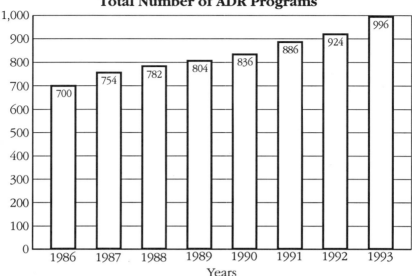

Years

Source: The Bank of New York, Depository Receipts (ADRs and GDRs), *1993 Market Review.*

Figure 5.
Total Number of Sponsored ADR Programs

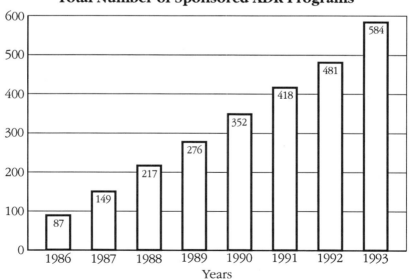

Years

Source: The Bank of New York, Depository Receipts (ADRs and GDRs), *1993 Market Review.*

Note: Excludes Rule 144A programs, Regulation S, and other private programs. In 1993, 24 new sponsored programs arose, 14 non-sponsored programs were converted into sponsored, and 38 sponsored programs were replaced by corporate stocks.

Figure 6.
Percentage of Total ADR Programs by Country

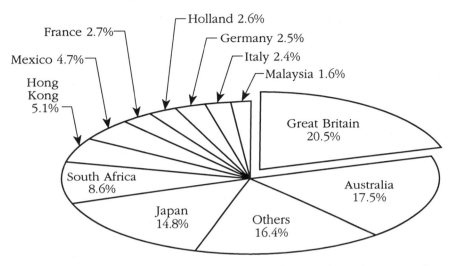

Source: The Bank of New York, Depository Receipts (ADRs and GDRs), *1993 Market Review*.

Figure 7.
Percentage of Sponsored ADR Programs by Country

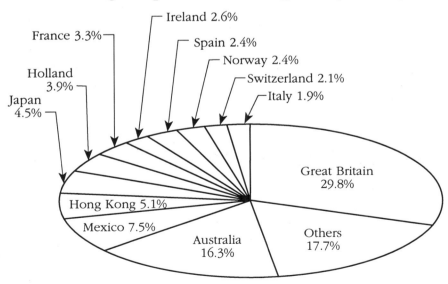

Source: The Bank of New York, Depository Receipts (ADRs and GDRs), *1993 Market Review*.

Figure 8.
Percentage of Dollar Volume of Depository Receipts
Traded by Country

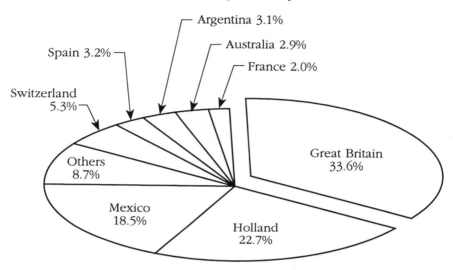

Source: The Bank of New York, Depository Receipts (ADRs and GDRs), *1993 Market Review.*

Note: Data on volume of depository receipts (ADRs and GDRs) listed on exchanges in 1993 is estimated on the basis of 256 of a total of 996 programs.

Figure 9.
Participation of Depository Banks in
Rule 144A DR Programs

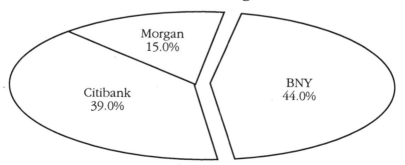

Source: The Bank of New York, Depository Receipts (ADRs and GDRs), *1993 Market Review.*

Note: Excludes Regulation S programs. As of December 31, 1993, there were 98 active Rule 144A programs.

Figure 10.
Bank Participation in New Sponsored Programs
Established in 1993

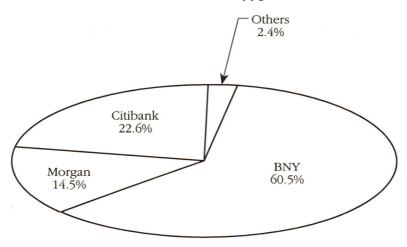

Source: The Bank of New York, Depository Receipts (ADRs and GDRs), *1993 Market Review.*

Figure 11.
Bank Participation in Sponsored Programs
Established in 1993

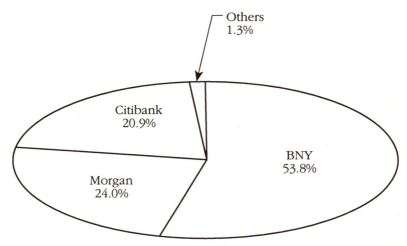

Source: The Bank of New York, Depository Receipts (ADRs and GDRs), *1993 Market Review.*

Figure 12.
Bank Participation in Converting Non-Sponsored
Programs into Sponsored Programs

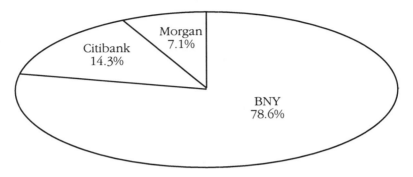

Source: The Bank of New York, Depository Receipts (ADRs and GDRs), *1993 Market Review.*

Figure 13.
Bank Participation in Programs Listed in 1993 on the NYSE,
AMEX, or NASDAQ

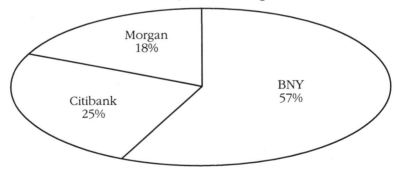

Source: The Bank of New York, Depository Receipts (ADRs and GDRs), *1993 Market Review.*

Notes

1. *Carta Financiera*, October 1992, 36.

2. International Finance Corporation, 1992, *Emerging Stock Markets Factbook 1992*. Washington, D.C.

Chapter 5

Chilean Pension Fund Reform
and its Impact on Savings

Erik Haindl Rondanelli

Abstract

Pension system reform is often argued to have an impact on long-run aggregate savings. The replacement of a state-run pay-as-you-go system by private fully funded schemes is claimed to raise aggregate savings and eliminate factor market distortions, therefore increasing long-term growth and welfare.

However, at a theoretical level, all these changes will have an uncertain impact on aggregate savings. Their impact will depend critically on individual perceptions, on the actuarial fairness of the pension schemes, on the existence of borrowing constraints, and on the pension fund financial balance.

This paper reviews the Chilean experience with pension fund reform and its impact on aggregate savings. Using econometric techniques, it is found that in the Chilean case, the implementation of a fully funded pension system in the 1980s had a positive impact on aggregate savings.

Pension System Reform

Pension system reform often is argued to have an impact on long-run aggregate savings. The replacement of a state-run pay-as-you-go system by private fully funded schemes is claimed to raise aggregate savings and eliminate factor market distortions, therefore increasing long-term growth and welfare.

However, at a theoretical level, all these changes will have an uncertain impact on aggregate savings. Their impact will depend critically on individual perceptions, on the actuarial fairness of the pension schemes, on the existence of borrowing constraints, and on the pension fund financial balance.

Even the introduction of a state-run pay-as-you-go pension system[1] in a situation without any social security at all may not affect long-run aggregate savings in a society. This situation will occur if individuals perceive that the social contributions they pay are, in fact, savings for their retirement and if, as a result, they reduce actual savings by the same amount of their social contributions, leaving the aggregate level of consumption intact. However, in the transition to a long-run situation, there probably will be an adverse effect on aggregate savings.[2]

In order for a pension reform to have a positive impact on aggregate savings in the long run, at least one of the following things should happen: People perceive their contributions under the current system as additional taxes, which will not be fully returned to them as pensions during retirement; some people have borrowing constraints and are forced to save for their future pension more than they wanted; at an individual level, pension payments are not matched by worker contributions; the pension system is not financially balanced.[3] The existence of most of these conditions is an empirical matter, so the impact of a pension reform on aggregate savings may differ between countries.

On the other hand, the introduction of a fully funded and earnings-related scheme in a situation without any social security also may leave aggregate savings unchanged. This will be the case in an economy formed by optimizing individuals with rational expectations, without borrowing constraints, and with voluntary savings that exceed mandatory savings. In this case, some of the conditions mentioned above should be present in order to have a positive impact on aggregate savings.

The replacement of a pay-as-you-go system for a fully funded pension system will have uncertain effects on aggregate savings. Many features will determine how substituting one scheme for another will affect the economy's macroeconomic variables including aggregate savings. Some features that will have critical macroeconomic effects in such a pension fund reform will be the following:[4]

1. *The distortionary nature of pay-as-you-go contributions.* Pay-as-you-go contributions are typically proportional to wages and therefore may distort labor market decisions if there is a weak link between workers' contributions and benefits. This link may be weak due to explicit income redistribution policies built into a pay-as-you-go pension system. For some workers, the benefits from this system will be less than their contributions, so the difference will be perceived as a tax. In an attempt to reduce the excess burden of the tax, some workers may reduce their supply of labor or shift into informal markets.

In addition, the average rates of return on contributions will differ from market interest rates. In a mature and balanced pay-as-you-go system with constant rate of population growth, pensioners are paid on average a real rate of return on their savings equal to the real rate of growth of the economy's wage bill. In a fully funded system, pensioners may receive the marginal productivity of capital as their rate of return on savings. This latter figure is always higher in a dynamically efficient economy. Otherwise, the economy would be to the right of the Golden Rule.[5]

Both effects will mean higher growth potential and welfare in a fully funded system. However, their impact on aggregate savings is uncertain.

2. *Myopia.* Myopia is the inability of adequately relating current pension contributions to old-age consumption. In the extreme myopic case, all workers see their full contribution as a pure tax, even when a fully funded system is introduced.In this case, the adoption of any mandatory scheme has similar distortionary consequences. However, the characteristics of a fully funded system that links benefits with contributions make myopia less likely to occur. Therefore, a switch from a pay-as-you-go system to a fully funded system may have a positive impact on welfare and growth. As before, the impact on aggregate savings is uncertain.

3. *Demographics.* A higher old-age dependency ratio, due to an older population or a lower retirement age, requires higher pay-as-you-go contributions and hence raises the macroeconomic and welfare effects of adopting such a scheme. A demographic transition toward an older population structure will imply increasing contributions to finance the pay-as-you-go system. By contrast, a fully funded system is independent of the old-age dependency ratio. Therefore, a switch from a pay-as-you-go system to a fully funded system will have a higher positive impact on welfare and growth when there is a higher old-age dependency ratio.

4. *Mandatory savings exceed initial voluntary savings.* When savings mandated by the compulsory pension system are lower than pre-system voluntary savings, adoption of a fully funded system implies that mandatory savings under the new system are fully offset by lower voluntary savings, and therefore the reform has no effects. However, when mandatory savings under the new system exceed initial voluntary savings, a fully funded scheme raises savings beyond voluntary levels, thus increasing aggregate savings of the economy.

A special case arises when a certain fraction of the population faces "borrowing constraints" and consumes all income. In this case, voluntary savings are equal to zero, and any mandatory savings scheme will have a substantial positive impact on aggregate savings.

5. *Voluntary intergenerational transfers.* If people are altruistic so that they leave bequests to their children, or children provide support to their aged parents, these voluntary intergenerational transfers can be adjusted to compensate for policy-induced intergenerational transfers, such as those imbedded in a pay-as-you-go system. Under extreme intergenerational altruism, the older generation leave higher bequests to their offspring, or children care less for their parents by an amount that exactly compensates for the young-to-old transfer of a pay-as-you-go system.

Under partial altruism, a pay-as-you-go system induces a net transfer of resources from the younger generations to the older ones. Since the marginal propensity to save of older generations is presumably lower than the marginal propensity to save of the working population, this transfer may imply a reduction in aggregate savings.

On the other hand, since a fully funded system lacks intergenerational distribution effects, the switch from a pay-as-you-go system to a fully funded system will probably have a positive impact on aggregate savings, as long as people are not extreme altruists.

6. *Financial openness of the economy.* Under strict financial openness and perfect integration to world markets, national savings decisions do not affect investment. Changes in savings impinge only on foreign asset holdings. Interest rates are determined exclusively by international rates. In a closed economy, however, changes in national savings affect investment and hence also affect the capital stock, the real interest rate, and the wage rate. A partially open financial market will produce intermediate results, with some effect on foreign asset holdings, some effect on interest rates, and some effect on the capital stock.

If aggregate savings rise as a consequence of a switch to a fully funded system in an economy with partially open financial markets, the probable outcome is an improved current account of the balance of payments (lower foreign assets holdings), an increase in the capital stock, a reduction in real interest rates, and an increase in real wages.

7. *Financing of system transition.* Perhaps the most important feature that influences aggregate savings is the way the transition is financed. The transition of a pay-as-you-go system to a fully funded system will imply that current workers will save for their future pensions. They cease to contribute to current pensioners. Therefore, the state takes the obligation to pay for the current pensions. This obligation induces a fiscal deficit that can be of considerable magnitude. The way the state finances this deficit is critical to the final macroeconomic outcome.

The straightforward way to finance the reform transition deficit is by issuing new government debt. The old implicit pay-as-you-go debt is swapped for new explicit government debt. Debt financing implies that the national savings, the capital stock, and the intergenerational distribution of welfare are only marginally affected by magnitudes that depend only on the net efficiency gains of the reform. Only implicit government debt is changed by an explicit government debt.

A very different result is obtained when the transition deficit is financed by raising taxes. Tax financing of the deficit is equivalent to combining the pension reform with a contractionary fiscal policy. A fully tax-financed transition hurts the tax-paying transition generation, which may include workers and current pensioners, and benefits non-taxed post-transition generations. Tax financing of the transition — as any restrictive fiscal policy that pays off government debt through taxes and hence shifts resources from current to future generations — encourages higher savings and capital formation.

Another possible restrictive fiscal policy is to finance the reform transition by reducing current government expenditures. This will hurt beneficiaries of these public expenditures but will benefit the rest of the population. The final result of such a policy may be a significant increase in aggregate savings and a huge accumulation of real capital.

8. *Financial balance of the pension system.* A pay-as-you-go system can be balanced financially, when pension payments are exactly matched by worker contributions. This is seldom the case; when pay-as-you-go systems are immature, they often show surpluses, and when they approach maturity, they often show losses. This is due to the rigidity in contribution rates applied to wage earnings. It is easy to find many developing countries, experiencing demographic transitions, that show significant losses in their pension fund systems.

On the other hand, a fully funded system is balanced almost by definition. Therefore, a switch of a mature pay-as-you-go system for a fully funded system will imply a reduction in the public deficit in the long run. This will have a positive impact on the economy's aggregate savings.

9. *Development of a capital market.* A pay-as-you-go system is a mandatory social contract of transfers from workers to pensioners. In order to implement these transfers, there is no need to accumulate financial or real capital. By contrast, a fully funded system is a mandatory savings system that forces workers to save part of their wage income for old age. The accumulated savings must be invested in financial and physical capital. Therefore, the implementation of a fully funded pension system generates a big demand for all kinds of financial assets and firm shares. This produces a financial deepening process that can be a decisive factor in order to develop a domestic capital market. This development should have a positive impact on aggregate savings.

Chilean Pension Reform

In 1980, Chile implemented a drastic pension reform, substituting the old pay-as-you-go system administered by the state for a fully funded privately managed system. Several privately managed pension funds emerged in 1980 in order to administer the workers' resources in a competitive framework, each of them competing on the basis of giving a higher rate of return to its affiliates and a better quality of service. Each registered person received a personal account where he or she could know the exact amount of its accumulated savings. Any person was free to move the account from one pension fund to another.

The government financed the reform transition by reducing its current expenditure and pursued a balanced budget policy. The privately managed pension funds were severely regulated in their portfolios and gradually were authorized to invest in a greater variety of financial assets.

The aggregate savings rate of the country increased from an average 16.7 percent of gross domestic product (GDP) in the pre-reform years (1976-1980) to an average 26.6 percent of GDP a decade after the reform (1990-1994). Of these 9.9 percentage points increase in the savings rate, a significant part may be attributed to the pension fund reform, as explained later. Table 1 shows the aggregate savings rate of the country as a percentage of GDP for the period 1974 to 1994.

Table 1.
Chile: Total Savings 1974 - 1994
%GDP

														Years							
	74	75	76	77	78	79	80	81	82	83	84	85	86	87	88	89	90	91	92	93	94
Private Savings																					
Pension Funds								0.9	2.0	1.8	1.8	1.7	1.8	1.8	2.7	2.9	2.9	3.0	3.1	3.3	3.4
Other	15.1	0.4	9.6	7.9	8.4	4.7	5.6	1.5	-2.8	6.0	7.9	5.3	7.6	11.8	13.7	12.9	15.7	15.9	15.5	15.1	16.3
Total Private Savings	15.1	0.4	9.6	7.9	8.4	4.7	5.6	2.4	-0.8	7.8	9.7	7.0	9.4	13.6	16.4	15.8	18.6	18.9	18.6	18.4	19.7
Public Savings																					
General Government	6.0	7.8	5.1	2.7	3.8	7.4	8.0	5.0	2.2	-2.2	-1.9	-0.5	1.0	2.5	5.1	7.2	4.9	4.4	5.4	4.8	4.9
Local Government	-0.4	-0.3	-0.2	0.1	0.4	0.3	0.3	0.3	0.1	0.0	-0.9	1.3	1.2	1.1	0.8	0.7	0.3	0.8	0.8	0.8	0.8
Total Public Savings	5.6	7.5	4.9	2.8	4.2	7.7	8.3	5.3	2.3	-2.2	-2.8	0.8	2.2	3.6	5.9	7.9	5.2	5.2	6.2	5.6	5.7
Domestic Savings	20.7	7.9	14.5	10.7	12.6	12.4	13.9	7.7	1.5	5.6	6.9	7.8	11.6	17.2	22.3	23.7	23.8	24.1	24.8	24.0	25.4
Foreign Savings	0.5	5.2	-1.7	3.7	5.2	5.4	7.1	14.3	9.5	5.6	10.8	9.4	7.3	5.0	0.5	1.8	2.0	0.4	2.0	4.8	1.4
Total Savings	**21.2**	**13.1**	**12.8**	**14.4**	**17.8**	**17.8**	**21.0**	**22.0**	**11.0**	**11.2**	**17.7**	**17.2**	**18.9**	**22.2**	**22.8**	**25.5**	**25.8**	**24.5**	**26.8**	**28.8**	**26.8**

Source: IMF, Central Bank, Inst. of Economics UGM

Of course, other major structural changes were implemented during this period, such as trade liberalization and financial deregulation and privatization, that also may have had an impact on savings, so the classical identification problem arises. In fact, the interaction of different structural reforms and foreign shocks makes it hard to disentangle the specific effects on savings that can be attributed to the pension reform. An attempt to measure the impact of the pension reform on the Chilean savings rate, with the help of a simple econometric model, is subsequently described.

The old pay-as-you-go pension system in Chile was administered by 32 different state institutions that financed old age pensioners with contributions from active workers, their employers, and the state. The biggest institutions were Servicio de Seguro Social (for blue-collar workers), Caja de Previsión de Empleados Particulares (for private white-collar workers), and Caja Nacional de Empleados Públicos y Periodistas (for public white-collar workers). These three institutions concentrated more than 94 percent of the 2.3 million affiliates in 1979, one year before the pension reform. Total registered persons represented around 68 percent of the labor force that year. Therefore, almost one-third of the labor force was not covered by the old pension system at all.

Social contributions varied by institution. Blue-collar workers (Servicio de Seguro Social) contributed with 36.2 percent of wages (7.25 percent paid directly by workers and 28.95 percent paid by employers). Of this amount, 22.95 percent of wages was allocated to pensions, and the remaining 13.25 percent was destined to health and other benefits. Private white-collar workers (Caja de Previsión de Empleados Particulares) contributed with 44.04 percent of wages (12.33 percent paid by employees and 31.71 percent paid by employers). Of this amount, 24.91 percent of wages was destined to pensions and the remainder to health and other benefits. Public white-collar workers (Caja Nacional de Empleados Públicos y Periodistas) contributed with 35.5 percent of wages (18.5 percent paid by employees and 17.0 percent paid by employers). Of this amount, 15.75 percent of wages was destined to pensions and the remainder for health and other benefits.

The old system was highly redistributive, so that pensions and other benefits paid had a weak link to actual contributions. Therefore, it is likely that these social contributions were regarded by most workers and employers as a tax on wages. As a consequence, labor market decisions were distorted severely with a corresponding loss in social welfare.

Even though the social contribution rates were high, the average pension paid was fairly low. In 1979, the average pension paid to a blue-collar pensioner was US$55 per month, which represented some 37.2 percent of per capita GDP. The average pension paid to a white-collar worker was US$83 per month (55.7 percent of per capita GDP) for the private sector and US$191 per month (128.2 percent of per capita GDP) for the public sector.

By contrast, under the new pension system, with lower social contributions, the average pension paid for all workers (blue-collar and white-collar) is substantially higher. In 1994, the average old age pension paid was US$163 per month, which represented 52.5 percent of per capita GDP.[6]

The old social security institutions in Chile generated a growing deficit. In 1979, the Chilean state transferred 2 percent of GDP in subsidies to cover the yearly deficit of the social security institutions. The combination of poorly administered social security institutions with a dramatic decline in the relation between active (contributing) and passive workers led the pay-as-you-go system to bankruptcy. In 1960, Chile had 10.8 active workers for each pensioner. Ten years later (1970), the relation had declined to 4.4. By 1979, the country had only 2.3 active workers for each pensioner.[7]

The new fully funded pension system was created in 1980. Eleven new private firms emerged to replace the old state social security institutions. The distinction between different categories of workers was abolished. Each worker could open a mandatory savings account in any firm (administradora de fondos de pensiones or AFP) and change his/her accumulated funds to another firm any time s/he wanted. Private pension funds (AFPs) had to compete with each other in order to get the preferences of the contributors. New workers were required to join the new system. Old workers could opt to join the new system or remain in the old one.

The new system implied a big reduction in social contribution rates. All workers were required to contribute 20.5 percent of their wages. Of this amount, 10 percent of wages went to an individual savings account administered by the AFPs; 7 percent of wages went to health institutions; and the remaining 3.5 percent was allocated to cover an insurance policy. A big incentive to join the new system was an approximate 10 percent increase in the workers' net wage, due to differences in social contribution rates.

Under the new scheme, once a worker reached retirement age (65 for males and 60 for females), s/he could get a pension from the AFP or could use his/her accumulated funds to buy a lifetime pension from an insurance company. There is a minimum guaranteed pension, so if accumulated savings for an individual are not enough to finance this minimum pension, the state makes up the difference.

The pension reform had ample success.[8] At the end of 1981, approximately 1.4 million workers (40 percent of the labor force) had joined the new system. By 1994, the total number of registered persons was 5.0 million (almost 95 percent of the labor force). Accumulated savings reached US$300 million (0.9 percent of GDP) at the end of 1981. At the end of 1994, accumulated savings represented more than US$22.4 billion (42.2 percent of GDP).

When the system was designed, a 4 percent estimated real rate of return on accumulated savings was used for the calculations. This would produce an average yearly pension equivalent to 70 percent of the last year's wages. The new pension fund system has generated an average effective rate of return of 13.5 percent in the period 1980-1994.

With this rate of return, workers can expect a pension that is significantly higher than the last wage.

Characteristics of the New Pension System

The new pension system started with 11 private firms in strong competition for the affiliates' resources. Total beneficiaries represented around 37 percent of the labor force in 1981-1982, of which around 70 percent were active contributors. During the following years, there was a clear upward trend in both registered and active contributors (see Table 2). At the end of 1994, registered persons represented almost 95 percent of the labor force, and active contributors made up 59 percent of that figure.

The number of pension firms also has increased, indicating a more competitive environment. The number of firms remained stable in the 1980s and increased dramatically in 1992 (see Table 2). At the end of 1994, there were 21 private pension firms. The share of the biggest three firms shows a clear downward trend during the whole period. In 1981, the biggest three firms concentrated 71.3 percent of all the pension funds. In 1994, this share declined to 52.7 percent (see Table 2).

The Herfindahl index[9] also shows increased competition levels. The index decreases from 0.217 in 1981, which is equivalent to almost five competing firms of the same size, to 0.126 in 1994, which is equivalent to almost eight competing firms of the same size.

Most of the competition in the market is through advertisement and sales efforts. Each firm has a large sales force that tries to capture its rivals' clientele. This effort explains the reduction in market concentration but means high costs for the pension funds. In fact, a puzzling result is that the average commission charged in dollar terms has increased during the years despite the higher number of firms (see Table 2).

The Superintendency of Pensions regulates this sector, especially in matters concerning pension fund portfolios. Only financial instruments approved by the authority could be eligible for investing the pension fund resources. Initially, only public bonds, bank deposits, housing mortgages, and selected firm bonds were allowed. In 1981, the pension fund portfolio had 62 percent of bank deposits and 28 percent of public bonds (see Table 3).

In 1986, pension funds were allowed to buy shares of firms. In 1993, pension funds were allowed to invest outside the country in high-grade financial instruments issued by some foreign governments. In 1994, pension funds received authorization to invest in bank bonds and investment funds. In 1994, the overall pension fund consisted of the following portfolio: 40 percent public bonds, 12 percent mortgages, 6 percent bank deposits, 5 percent firm bonds, and almost 34 percent shares (see Table 3).

Over time, the increased investment opportunities produced a significant real rate of return on the pension fund. The average real rate of return for the 1980-1994 period reached 13.5 percent. The maximum rate of return was 28.8 percent in 1982, and the minimum rate of return was 3.1 percent in 1992 (according to the Superintendency of Pensions).

Table 2.
Chile: Some Characteristics of the Pension System

	1981	1982	1983	1984	1985	1986	1987
Registered							
Number	1,400,000	1,440,000	1,620,000	1,930,000	2,283,830	2,591,484	2,890,680
% Labor Force	36.7	37.4	40.7	46.5	53.7	60.1	65.8
Active Contributors							
Number	NA	1,060,000	1,230,000	1,558,194	1,774,057	2,023,739	2,167,568
% Beneficiaries	NA	73.6	75.9	80.7	77.7	78.1	75.0
Numbers of Firms	12	12	12	12	11	12	12
Concentration Ratio							
Share Biggest 3	71.3	67.6	65.7	65.4	65.8	66.6	66.7
Herfindahl Index	0.217	0.194	0.180	0.174	0.179	0.182	0.178
Average Commission							
US$ per Contribution	NA	45	33	25	15	13	12
% of Fund	NA	8.5	4.4	3.0	1.9	1.4	1.1
Pension Fund Size							
Million US$	305	606	1,136	1,244	1,532	2,117	2,707
% of GDP	0.9	3.7	6.5	8.5	10.6	12.7	14.2

	1988	1989	1990	1991	1992	1993	1994
Registered							
Number	3,183,002	3,470,845	3,739,542	4,109,184	4,434,795	4,708,840	5,014,444
% Labor Force	69.9	74.2	79.1	85.7	88.9	90.2	94.6
Active Contributors							
Number	2,267,622	2,642,757	2,486,813	2,695,580	2,695,580	2,792,118	2,943,479
% Beneficiaries	71.2	76.1	66.5	65.6	60.8	59.3	58.7
Numbers of Firms	13	13	14	13	19	20	21
Concentration Ratio							
Share Biggest 3	66.3	65.3	62.6	59.0	56.6	54.4	52.7
Herfindahl Index	0.172	0.168	0.158	0.147	0.138	0.130	0.126
Average Commission							
US$ per Contribution	75	77	79	90	113	123	135
% of Fund	5.4	4.9	3.3	2.8	2.6	2.4	2.1
Pension Fund Size							
Million US$	3,585	4,470	6,655	10,064	12,395	15,942	22,435
% of GDP	15.1	17.8	24.4	31.4	30.6	37.0	42.2

Source: Superintendency of Pensions, Institute of Economics UGM.

Table 3.
Chile: Pension Fund Portfolio
% of the Fund

	1981	1982	1983	1984	1985	1986	1987
Public Bonds (%)	28.1	26.0	44.5	42.2	42.6	46.7	41.5
Mortgage Bonds	9.4	46.8	50.6	43.1	35.3	25.5	21.4
Bank Deposits	61.9	26.6	2.7	12.9	20.9	23.2	28.3
Firm Bonds	0.6	0.6	2.2	1.8	1.2	0.8	2.6
Shares							
Foreign Investment							
Bank Bonds							
Investment Funds						3.8	6.2
Total	100.0	100.0	100.0	100.0	100.0	100.0	100.0
Real Return	*12.6*	*28.8*	*21.3*	*3.5*	*13.4*	*12.3*	*5.4*
	1988	1989	1990	1991	1992	1993	1994
Public Bonds (%)	35.4	41.6	44.1	34.7	40.9	39.4	39.7
Mortgage Bonds	20.6	17.7	16.1	12.1	14.3	13.1	12.4
Bank Deposits	29.5	21.5	17.4	12.0	11.0	7.5	6.3
Firm Bonds	6.4	9.1	11.1	9.6	9.2	7.0	5.2
Shares	8.1	10.1	11.3	31.6	24.6	32.5	34.3
Foreign Investment						0.5	0.4
Bank Bonds							1.3
Investment Funds							0.4
Total	100.0	100.0	100.0	100.0	100.0	100.0	100.0
Real Return	*6.4*	*6.9*	*15.5*	*29.7*	*3.1*	*16.2*	*18.2*

Source: Superintendency of Pensions, Institute of Economics UGM.

A Model for the Savings Rate

The aggregate savings rate of Chile can be divided into the following components:

$$S = Sp + Spen + Sg + Se$$

where:

- S: aggregate savings
- Sp: private savings
- Spen: mandatory savings in private pension funds
- Sg: government savings (includes state social security)
- Se: external savings

External savings (Se) correspond to the deficit in the current account of the balance of payments. This variable is the result of the interaction of the desired foreign net capital inflow (an exogenous variable to the country) and the Central Bank desire to accumulate foreign reserves (a policy variable) interacting with all sorts of regulations to the capital inflow (also a policy variable). In the period 1974-1994, external savings represented 4.8 percent of GDP on average, with a maximum of 14.3 percent of GDP in 1981 and a minimum of -1.7 percent of GDP in 1976.

Government savings (Sg) correspond to the difference between government incomes and current expenditures. This is a policy variable. In the period 1974-1994, government savings represented 4.4 percent of GDP on average, with a maximum of 8.3 percent of GDP in 1980 and a minimum of -2.8 percent of GDP in 1984.

Mandatory savings in private pension funds (Spen) is equal to 10 percent of the wage base by definition. This is a variable with a clear upward trend. In the period 1981-1994, mandatory savings in private pension funds averaged 1.6 percent of GDP, with a maximum of 3.4 percent of GDP in 1994 and a minimum of 0.9 percent of GDP in 1981.

Private savings (Sp) is a more complex variable to model. In the period 1974-1994, it had an extremely mutable behavior, with an average of 9.3 percent of GDP, and a maximum of 16.3 percent of GDP in 1994 and a minimum of -2.8 percent of GDP in 1982. This variable reflects private sector behavior and constraints. There are several competing theories that try to explain private savings in terms of observed variables, and each of them puts some emphasis on different factors. An eclectic approach would let the data decide what factor is important for the Chilean case. Some important considerations are the following:

- Almost all saving theories make emphasis on the importance of disposable income as an explanatory variable. A higher disposable income normally is associated with higher private savings. As a consequence, every variable that affects disposable income will have an impact on private savings.
- The first variable that affects disposable income is taxes. A higher tax burden means lower disposable income, and therefore, people have to reduce either consumption, savings, or both. The specific incidence on private consumption depends on this decision. The tax burden is therefore an important explanatory variable of the private savings rate.
- The second variable is net foreign income. Higher net foreign income also means lower disposable income for a given value of GDP. This variable is defined as net foreign factor payments less unrequited transfers and, in the case of Chile, is strongly influenced by interest payments on the foreign debt.
- Another important consideration is the existence of a fraction of the population that experiences borrowing constraints. For that population, observed income is the relevant explanatory variable, as in

the standard Keynesian case. For the rest of the population, the capital market allows complete consumption smoothing, and hence the relevant variable is permanent income. In order to capture the influence on private savings of consumers with borrowing constraints, a variable that measures transitory income was constructed. This variable was defined as the ratio of permanent to observed income.[10] According to the permanent income hypothesis, all transitory income is saved. On the other hand, consumers with borrowing constraints may not save anything out of transitory income. Hence, this variable will capture the empirical relevance of these constrained consumers.

- The classical theory of savings emphasizes the role of the real interest rate in influencing intertemporal consumption. Therefore, the real interest rate is a natural explanatory variable. For the Chilean case, the real interest rate paid on deposits in the banking system is used as an explanatory variable.

- Mandatory savings on private pension funds may crowd out all or part of the other private savings, as was discussed before. Therefore, mandatory savings should be a variable in order to measure if this crowding-out effect exists or not.

- Foreign savings also may have a crowding-out effect on private savings. There is some international evidence on the existence of this crowding-out effect at least for Colombia and Bolivia.[11] Some of the increased foreign savings may end up financing additional consumption. Therefore, foreign savings is used as an explanatory variable.

- Public savings also may have some crowding-out effect on private savings. A World Bank study of a sample of developing countries found that less than one-half of the increase in public savings obtained by cutting government consumption will be offset by lower private savings.[12] In order to see if this effect is present in the Chilean case, public savings is used as an explanatory variable.

- Pension funds have been decisive in the development of capital markets. This financial deepening process can be an important factor in order to induce higher private savings. The size of the pension fund is used to measure the influence of this financial deepening process on private savings.

Chilean private savings are modeled as a linear function of all previous variables, expressed as a percentage of GDP. The econometric model used is the following:

$$Sp = a0 + a1*TAX + a2*NFP + a3*Qperm + a4*Spen + a5*Sg +$$

$$a6*Se + a7*SIZE + a8*Rint + e$$

where:

TAX: total tax burden (percent of GDP)

NFP: net foreign factor payments less unrequited transfers (percent of GDP)

Qperm: ratio of permanent income to observed income

SIZE: size of the pension fund (percent of GDP)

Rint: real interest rate paid on deposits

e: error term

Total savings of the country are the sum of all components:

$$S = Sp + Spen + Sg + Se$$

and combining both equations:

$$S = a0 + a1^*TAX + a2^*NFP + a3^*Qperm + (1+a4)^*Spen + (1+a5)^*Sg$$

$$+ (1+a6)^*Se + a7^*SIZE + a8^*Rint + e$$

Since total savings are equal to total investment (at least in an ex-post sense), an additional equation (not shown) relating investment to the real interest rate and other relevant variables is implicit in the analysis. Modeling this simultaneous equation system is beyond the scope of this paper, since it would bring additional complexities into the analysis.[13]

All macroeconomic variables defined above are expressed as a fraction of GDP. Therefore, all variables are stationary almost by definition. This removes the possibility of having spurious regression problems and eliminates the need to perform cointegration analysis.

Table 4 presents the estimated coefficients using ordinary least squares (OLS) and two-stage least squares (TSLS) techniques for Sp. Since interest rate is probably an endogenous variable, a standard simultaneous equation bias may result from OLS estimation. Therefore, TSLS is used to solve this simultaneous equation bias.[14] Parameters are robust to different estimation techniques. The third regression uses only significant variables. The main results are the following:

1. The model is very good in tracking most of the variation in private savings. Almost 95 percent of the total variation is explained by these variables (see Figure 1).

2. The total tax burden (TAX) has a significant influence on private savings. A higher tax burden means lower private savings. The estimated coefficient exceeds one, although a null hypothesis of one cannot be rejected by the data. In fact, a one standard deviation confidence interval would give a range of -0.92 to -1.63 for this coefficient. This implies that probably most of the tax increases are financed through a reduction in private savings.

Table 4.
Chile: Private Savings
t-Statistic Values in Parentheses

Variable	Regression 1 (OLS)	Regression 2 (TSLS)	Regression 3 (OLS)
Constant	65.0521	64.4395	67.4959
	(8.2639)	(7.2579)	(10.5602)
Tax	-1.2647	-1.2768	-1.5304
	(-3.6842)	(-3.6093)	(-6.4001)
NFP	-0.4605	-0.4290	-0.4584
	(-2.0539)	(-1.3985)	(-3.9943)
QPERM	-24.3805	-23.8166	-23.3128
	(-4.2588)	(-3.4777)	(-4.6862)
Spen	-0.1198	-0.2261	
	(-0.1082)	(-0.1720)	
Sg	-0.1011	-0.0904	
	(-0.6249)	(-0.5108)	
Se	-0.1271	-0.1389	
	(-0.8368)	(-0.8189)	
Pension Fund Size	0.1172	0.1258	0.0990
	(1.3433)	(1.2038)	(2.3762)
RINT	-0.1740	-0.1452	
	(-1.8561)	(-0.6838)	
R-squared	0.9569	0.9566	0.9341
Adjusted R-squared	0.9282	0.9276	0.9176
S.E. of regression	1.5096	1.5155	1.6168
Durbin-Watson stat	2.4464	2.4335	2.2366
Sum of squared res	27.3452	27.5606	41.8257
F-Statistic	33.3364	33.0642	56.7351

Period: 1974 - 1994
Source: Author's calculations.

Figure 1.
Private Savings
% of GDP

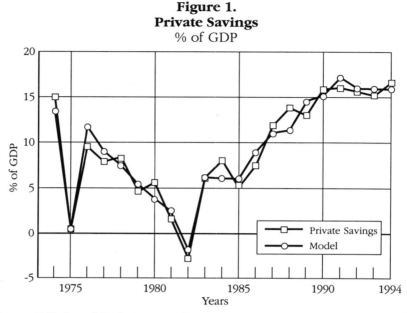

Source: IMF, Central Bank, Institute of Economics UGM.

3. Net foreign factor payments (NFP) present also a significant influence on private savings. There is a negative coefficient of -0.43 to -0.46, depending on the regression.

This means that for an increase in net foreign factor payments equivalent to 1 percent of GDP (due to higher interest payments on foreign debt, for example), private savings are reduced in -0.43 to -0.46 percent of GDP and private consumption in the remaining difference.

4. Transitory income also exerts a significant influence on private savings. The extreme version of permanent income hypothesis is rejected by the data,[15] probably reflecting the existence of borrowing constraints for a significant fraction of the population. This fraction of the population reacts only to observed income.

5. Using the second regression (TSLS), it is found that for each increase in permanent income equivalent to 1 percent of GDP, private savings are increased in 0.41 percent of GDP and private consumption in the remaining 0.59 percent of GDP. On the other hand, an increase in transitory income by the same amount would induce a rise in private savings in 0.64 percent of GDP and a rise in private consumption in the remaining 0.36 percent of GDP.

6. The previous figures suggest that the consumers facing borrowing constraints represent more than one-third of total income in Chile. Assuming that constrained consumers belong to the lowest levels of

income, and using the income distribution calculated in CASEN studies,[16] it is found that almost 70 percent of the households would be in this situation. Probably, the first seven deciles of the income distribution face borrowing constraints and spend almost all their actual incomes in consumption. The top three deciles would do almost all the private savings of the country and may follow the permanent income hypothesis behavior.

7. The coefficient a4 captures the pension fund mandatory savings influence on voluntary private savings. It reflects the existence or nonexistence of a direct crowding-out effect of these mandatory savings. If mandatory savings are fully offset by lower voluntary savings, this coefficient would be -1. On the other hand, if voluntary savings are not affected by mandatory savings, this coefficient would be 0. The results indicate a small crowding-out effect (between -0.12 and -0.23, depending on the regression), which is consistent with a big part of the population facing borrowing constraints. However, results are not conclusive. A null hypothesis of no crowding out (a4=0) or of complete crowding out (a4= -1) cannot be rejected by the data.

8. The coefficient a5 measures the crowding-out effect of government savings on private savings. A full Ricardian equivalence would produce a coefficient of -1. A reduction in government savings would be perceived as meaning higher taxes in the future, and people would increase private savings now in anticipation of the future tax rise. On the other hand, a coefficient of 0 would mean no crowding out. The results indicate a small crowding-out effect (around -0.10), but the coefficient is not significant. A null hypothesis of no crowding out (a5=0) cannot be rejected by the data. However, a null hypothesis of a full Ricardian equivalence (a5= -1) is strongly rejected by the data.

9. The coefficient a6 measures the impact of external savings on private savings. An increase in external savings means higher foreign resources available for either investment or consumption. The coefficient a6 indicates what fraction of these increased resources actually is used to finance investment and what fraction actually is used to finance a higher level of consumption. A coefficient of 0 indicates that all the increase in external savings is used to finance a higher level of investment. A coefficient of -1 indicates that all increased foreign resources finance higher levels of consumption. Regression results indicate a small crowding-out effect (around -0.13), but the coefficient is not significant. A null hypothesis of no crowding out, which implies that all foreign resources are used to finance higher investment, cannot be rejected by the data.

10. The size of the pension fund is exerting a positive influence on private savings. This probably reflects the financial deepening effects induced by a bigger pension fund as well as the development of a more sophisticated capital market.

11. The real interest rate is not a significant variable and has a negative sign. The hypothesis of a zero interest rate elasticity is accepted by the data, indicating that this market is inelastic. On the other hand, the negative

values for the elasticity could also be explained by an income effect that systematically exceeds the substitution effect. Since almost all the savings is done by the upper deciles, they would probably be net leaders. Therefore, an increase in the real interest rate would produce a positive wealth effect that stimulates consumption.

Conclusion

Chile has experienced a substantial increase in the total savings rate during the last two decades (1974-1994). One significant factor that explains part of this increase is the pension fund reform. From the pre-reform years (1976-1980) to the post-reform years (1990-1994), the total savings rate of the country increased by more than 9.9 percentage points of GDP, from 16.7 to 26.6 percent. The model elaborated before can be used to explain the cause of this increase. This is done using regression number two (see Table 5).

Table 5.
Chile: Explanation of the Increase in Total Savings
% GDP

	Pre-Reform 1976-80	Post-Reform 1990-94	Change in Variable	Effect on Savings
Private Savings				
Tax Burden	24.2	19.6	-4.6	5.9
Net Factor Payment	2.4	3.8	1.4	-0.6
Ratio Per/Obs.	0.94	1.0	0.06	-1.4
Pension Savings	0.0	3.1	3.1	-0.7
External Savings	3.9	2.1	-1.8	0.2
Fund Size	0.0	33.1	33.1	4.2
Real Interest	12.9	6.6	-6.3	0.9
Residual Factor				0.0
Private Savings	7.2	15.7	8.5	8.5
Pension Savings	0.0	3.1	3.1	3.1
Public Savings	5.6	5.7	0.1	0.1
External Savings	3.9	2.1	-1.8	-1.8
Total Savings	**16.7**	**26.6**	**9.9**	**9.9**

Source: Author's calculations.

From Table 5, it is apparent that the pension fund reform explains an increase in total savings of 6.6 percentage points of GDP. This is the result of the pension savings (3.1 percent of GDP), the fund size effect (4.2 percent of GDP), and the small crowding out of pension savings (-0.7 percent of GDP). Hence, two-thirds of the increase in total savings of the country during this period can be attributed to the pension fund reform.

The pension reform not only increased total savings by such a significant amount but also implied a mayor reform for the Chilean capital market. The pension fund size became an important part of the economy, and its demand for new financial instruments generated an important capital deepening process. The increased competition between pension firms improved the efficiency of the capital market, implying a better resource allocation of the country savings.

Even though the pension fund portfolios are strictly regulated on diversification and risk issues, the real rate of return earned by the system since its creation looks impressive: 13.5 percent. This implies that not only the absolute level of savings was important but also that its productivity was high. Consequently, the contribution of these funds to the overall growth of the country was also high.

The role of the public sector was very important in achieving increased savings in the country. In fact, the government paid the pensioners remaining in the old system with its own resources, without receiving new contributions from the incoming labor force. This generated a potential deficit of 4.6 percentage points of GDP during 1990-1994. The public sector was able to reduce other current expenditures in order to accommodate this deficit and even increase public savings.

Had the public sector just decreased its savings by 4.6 percentage points of GDP, by making no efforts to accommodate this potential deficit, total savings of the country would have been lower by 4.2 percentage points of GDP in the period 1990-1994. Total savings of the country would have been only 22.4 percent of GDP in 1994-1996 instead of 26.6 percent of GDP. Even in this case, the pension fund reform still would have a positive impact in overall savings, although the absolute impact would have been reduced to only 2.2 percentage points of GDP.

The reduction in the tax burden is the other single measure that increased total savings. This factor helped to offset some negative developments in net foreign factor payments and the reduction of external savings.

Notes

1. In a pay-as-you-go system, workers contribute a fraction of their wages in order to finance actual pensions. In principle, no fund is needed to finance a pay-as-you-go system, since only a redistribution between generations takes place. By contrast, in a fully funded system, every worker has a savings account, and the pension is paid out of accumulated savings. This scheme requires a fund in order to finance the pension payments.

2. Of course, the short-run impact could reduce aggregate savings, since the first generation will receive a pension (higher income) without any past savings. They will enjoy an increased level of consumption, thus reducing aggregate savings.

3. In this case, the public sector surplus (deficit) is changed, which will have an impact on aggregate savings provided that the economy does not show a Ricardian equivalence.

4. For a more detailed discussion, see Corsetti and Schmidt-Hebbel 1994, 2-8.

5. This is a well-known proposition from growth theory. In the Golden Rule, per capita consumption is maximized in the steady state. This requires that marginal productivity of capital is equal to the rate of growth of the labor force. To be at the right of this point is a dynamically inefficient over-accumulation of capital that reduces steady state welfare.

6. The new pension system average for blue- and white-collar workers is comparable to the previous average for white-collar workers. As the blue collars earn less than white collars, this is an improvement.

7. Cheyre 1988, 69.

8. Even though the new pension system was implemented at the time of the foreign debt crisis, the pension funds did not suffer any economic losses. In macroeconomic conditions, they played no role in the crisis, since the fiscal sector had big surpluses at the time and did not use foreign debt to finance the system transition.

9. The Herfindahl index is defined as $H = \sum s_i^2$, where s_i is the market share of firm i. Its inverse is usually interpreted as the number of equivalent equal size competing firms.

10. This ratio is equal to one whenever transitory income is zero. With positive transitory income (booms), the ratio is less than one, and with negative transitory income (recessions), the ratio is bigger than one.

11. See, for example, Shome et al. 1995, 53; and The World Bank 1991, 122.

12. The World Bank 1991, 122-123.

13. If a Keynesian framework is used to model the investment-savings interaction with the rest of the economy, a complete model of the Chilean economy would be required.

14. Public investment was used as an instrumental variable.

15. This is tested using a null hypothesis that ao = 100 (all transitory income is saved). The t test is -4.43988, which implies a rejection of the null hypothesis at a 5 percent confidence level.

16. Encuesta de Caracterizacion Socioeconomica Nacional (CASEN) for 1985, 1987, 1990, 1992. See Haindl and Weber 1987 and Haindl, Budinich, and Irarrázaval 1989.

References

Cheyre, Hernán. 1988. "La Previsión en Chile: Ayer y Hoy." *Centro de Estudios Públicos*, July.

Cifuentes, Rodrigo. 1993. "Reformando los Sistemas Previsionales: Macroeconomía y Bienestar." Manuscript presented at the Econometric Society at Tucumán, August.

Corsetti, Giancarlo, and Klaus Schmidt-Hebbel. 1994. "Pension Reform and Growth." Manuscript presented at the Conference on Pensions: Funding and Macroeconomic Policy at Santiago, January.

Haindl, Erik, and Karl Weber. 1987. "Impacto Redistributivo del Gasto Social." *Departamento de Economía Universidad de Chile*, Serie de Investigación No. 79.

Haindl, Erik, Emita Budinich, and Ignacio Irarrázaval. 1989. "Gasto Social Efectivo." *Oficina de Planificación Nacional.*

Iglesias, Augusto, and Rodrigo Acuña. 1988. "Proyección de los Fondos de Pensiones." In *Centro de Estudios Públicos* chapter of "Sistema Privado de Pensiones en Chile" edited by Baeza and Manubens.

Shome, Parthasarathi, David Dunn, Erik Haindl, Arnold Harberger, and Osvaldo Schenone. 1995. "Comprehensive Tax Reform: The Colombian Experience." *IMF Occasional Paper No. 123.*

World Bank. 1991. "World Development Report 1991." New York: Oxford University Press.

Chapter 6

Foreign Direct Investment in Latin America

Robert Grosse

Abstract

Foreign direct investment (FDI) in Latin America has proved to be an important engine of growth during the first half of the 1990s. In most years, FDI flows do not exceed foreign bank loans or foreign portfolio investment, but FDI is more stable and less likely to flee countries during times of crisis. While not generally constituting a very large percentage of total capital formation in most countries, FDI still plays an important role in the development of the economies of these countries. FDI correlates strongly with local capital investment and may be seen as an indicator of confidence in an economy that tends to draw with it more capital investment from local sources.

Foreign direct investment appears to be driven largely by market size in Latin America, as has been demonstrated repeatedly in the literature, for various geographic regions and globally, over the years. In addition, factors such as per capita income, a country's fiscal balance, and the available rate of return on investment all contribute positively to attract FDI. Perceived riskiness of a country and a higher international price of oil showed strong negative impacts on the flow of FDI into Latin America.

FDI demonstrates a strong complementary relationship to local capital investment, rather than possibly substituting for it. Moreover, FDI shows almost no relationship to domestic savings in Latin America, so that other factors appear to drive those investment decisions. This last finding is positive in that domestic savings do not have to be increased in order to attract FDI but puzzling in that both domestic and foreign investment are expected to correlate positively with domestic savings. The savings puzzle is explored in other chapters in this volume.

Introduction

P rivate sector foreign investment has been the largest source of external finance provided to Latin American countries during the first half of the 1990s. It has far outstripped the traditional financing sources of cross-border bank loans and government and multilateral organization assistance. Private foreign investment can be divided into that which occurs to pursue rates of return on securities (that is, portfolio investment) and that which occurs to control company activities (direct investment). In the past decade, portfolio investment flows were exceeded by direct investments, but the demand by investors to diversify their portfolios into emerging market securities pushed portfolio investment ahead of FDI during the 1990s. A comparison of the values of different forms of foreign finance in Latin America is depicted in Figure 1.

Direct investment involves the establishment of a new company or the purchase of an existing company, in total or in part, such that the foreign firm asserts some degree of managerial control over the local affiliate. From purchases of formerly state-owned companies such as the airline LanChile in Chile (by the Spanish airline Iberia) and the telephone company ENTel in Argentina (in two parts, by consortia including Bell Atlantic in one case and Telefonica de España in the other) to *de novo* investments by Black & Decker in Mexico and Ford in Brazil, foreign multinational firms have moved into or grown extensively in the region during the past few years.

Figure 1.
Foreign Financial Flows into Latin America (US$ millions)

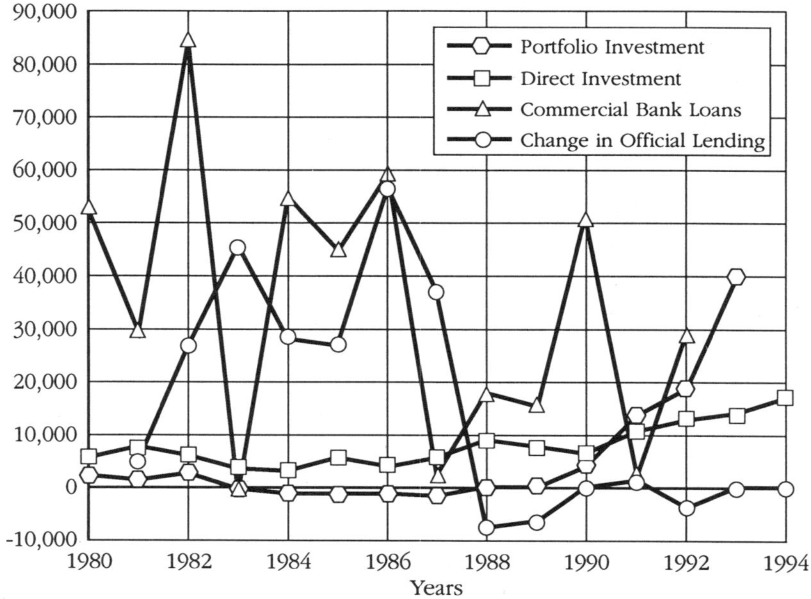

Source: World Bank, Interamerican Development Bank, Bank for International Settlements.

The regulatory environment has loosened, and public opinion vis-à-vis multinational enterprises has improved to the point where foreign firms now are competing widely with their domestic counterparts in almost every country of Latin America. This reality is virtually a complete reversal of the conditions in the 1970s, when most countries of the region were highly protectionist and broadly anti-foreign, and the 1980s, when the region fell into an external debt crisis that all but eliminated foreign direct investment and foreign bank lending alike.[1]

Indeed, the rapid growth of foreign direct investment into Latin American countries in the early 1990s can be traced at least partially to specific legislative changes related to foreign firms operating there. In the case of Argentina, the policy of privatization has led directly to foreign (and domestic) purchases of formerly state-owned enterprises in industries ranging from electric power to railroads, from telephones to oil and gas. Foreign investors' purchases of controlling interest in the national telephone system alone accounted for over $3 billion of FDI into that country in 1990. In the cases of Chile and Mexico, debt conversion programs have allowed foreign direct investors to buy the government's external commercial bank debt in the secondary market and convert that debt into ownership of local companies, sometimes in the process of privatization as well. Debt conversions in Chile have been estimated to account for over $3 billion of FDI during the period 1987-1990.[2]

How extensive has this about-face been? To what does the turnaround owe its existence? How has foreign direct investment contributed to capital formation in Latin America? How does it relate to domestic savings in the region? These are the issues that are explored below. The reality of booming foreign direct investment in Latin America — continuing even after the Mexican financial crisis of December 1994 — is hard to explain, given three prior decades of restrictions on that investment and economic conditions often unfavorable to it. The subsequent question as to whether FDI adds to total investment and capital formation, or largely replaces some of it, also needs to be considered carefully.

Historical Trends of FDI in Latin America

Foreign direct investment is not new to Latin America in the 1990s, nor even in the 1980s or 1970s. The first major investments in the post-colonial period were undertaken during the 1820s,[3] mainly in mining ventures such as gold and silver in Mexico, Peru, and Chile. Additional waves of direct investment (and greater amounts of portfolio investment) that occurred throughout the last century generally focused on raw materials, such as minerals and metals, as well as farming. In the last few decades of the century, investments in building and operating railroads and telegraph lines also became important, especially in Mexico and Argentina.[4] During this period, British direct investment far outweighed that from any other source country; U.S. FDI was limited largely to agricultural ventures in Cuba and railroads, mines, and oil in Mexico.[5] Table 1 shows the value of foreign direct investment in selected countries of the region at the beginning of World War I.

Table 1.
Latin America: Foreign Private Investment at
the End of 1914 (US$m)[a]

	Creditor Countries					
Debtor Countries	United Kingdom	France	Germany	United States	Others	Total
Argentina[b]	1,502	289	235	40	1,151	3,217
Bolivia[c]	17	25	...	2	...	44
Brazil	609	391	...	50	146	1,196
Chile[d]	216	...	89	558	...	494
Colombia	31	1	...	21	1	54
Costa Rica	3	...	...	41	...	44
Dominican Republic	0	...	...	11	...	11
Ecuador	29	2	...	9	...	40
El Salvador	6	...	...	7	2	15
Guatemala	44	...	12	36	...	92
Haiti	0	...	...	10	...	10
Honduras	1	...	...	15	...	16
Mexico	635	...	...	542	...	1,177
Nicaragua	2	...	...	4	...	6
Panama	0	...	...	23	...	23
Paraguay	18	...	...	5	...	23
Peru[d]	121	1	...	58	...	180
Uruguay	154	...	2	0	199	355
Subtotal	*3,385*	*709*	*305*	*1,099*	*1,499*	*6,997*
Venezuela	30	2	15	38	60	145
Subtotal II	*3,415*	*711*	*320*	*1,137*	*1,559*	*7,142*
Cuba	170	...	...	216	...	386
Subtotal III	*3,585*	*711*	*320*	*1,353*	*1,559*	*7,528*
Undistributed by debtor country	—	—	—	41	—	41
Total	**3,585**	**711**	**320**	**1,394**	**1,559**	**7,569**

Source: United Nations 1965, Table 17.

a = The figures in European or Latin American currencies have been converted into dollars on the basis of the gold exchange par at the end of 1914. The figures correspond to the amounts outstanding on December 31 unless otherwise indicated.

b = Outstanding amount as of December 31, 1918.

c = Outstanding amount as of December 31, 1917.

d = Outstanding amount as of December 31, 1915.

... = Values not available.

Foreign direct investment became more frequent a vehicle of foreign finance in Latin America during the inter-war period (1919-1939). Large U.S. and some European multinational companies such as Singer, ITT, Exxon, United Fruit, and others built extensive affiliate networks in Latin America, generally focusing on the larger countries — Argentina, Brazil, and Mexico. A sectoral distribution of U.S. FDI activities in Latin America in this period is presented in Table 2.

Table 2.
United States: Direct Investment in Latin America by Sector, 1897-1929
(aggregate totals in US$m at end of year)

Economic Sector	1897 Total	%	1908 Total	%	1914 Total	%	1919 Total	%	1924 Total	%	1929 Total	%
Agriculture	56.5	18.6	158.2	21.1	238.5	18.7	500.1	25.3	830.6	30.0	877.3	24.1
Sugar	24.0		57.0		115.0		354.0		688.0		643.5	
Fruit	8.5		28.2		57.5		67.1		86.1		153.8	
Others	24.0		73.0		66.0		79.0		76.5		80.0	
Mining and smelting	79.0	26.0	302.6	40.4	552.2	43.3	660.8	33.4	713.0	25.7	801.4	22.0
Precious ores & stones	58.0		141.6		176.2		145.5		151.0		164.3	
Industrial minerals	21.0		161.0		376.0		516.3		562.0		637.6	
Petroleum	10.5	3.5	68.0	9.1	130.0	10.2	326.0	16.5	533.0	19.2	731.5	20.1
Production	3.5		55.0		107.0		286.0		473.0		654.0	
Distribution	7.0		13.0		23.0		40.0		60.0		77.5	
Railroads	129.7	42.6	110.0	14.7	175.7	13.8	211.2	10.7	261.3	9.4	230.1	6.3
Public utilities	10.1	3.3	51.5	6.9	98.4	78.7	101.0	5.1	161.9	5.8	575.9	15.8
Manufacturing	3.0	1.0	30.3	4.0	37.0	2.9	84.0	4.2	127.0	4.6	231.0	6.3
Trade	13.5	4.4	23.5	3.1	33.5	2.6	71.0	3.6	93.0	3.3	119.2	3.3
Others	2.0	0.6	5.0	0.7	10.5	0.8	23.5	1.2	59.5	2.0	79.4	2.2
Total	304.3	100	748.8	100	1,275.8	100	1,977.6	100	2,779.3	100	3,645.8	100

Source: United Nations 1965, Table 15.

After World War II, the amount of foreign direct investment into Latin America began to take off, as it did in Western Europe. Much of this investment was by U.S.-based companies, though again some of it came from larger European multinationals. Data on the volumes of FDI from different countries and into different industries are generally difficult to obtain, except for that of U.S. companies. Tables 3 and 4 show the direct investment flows from U.S. firms and from total foreign firms in selected Latin American countries during the period from 1950 to 1994.

Table 3.
U.S. FDI Capital Outflows in Latin America, 1950-1994
(US$ millions)

Year	1950	1955	1960	1965	1970	1975	1980	1985	1990	1993
Total LA	154	141	95	171	696	1,215	2,755	4,364	3,392	7,817
Argentina	27	8	70	992	42	-58	629	73	164	939
Brazil	56	22	83	1,073	106	332	337	16	1,054	3,304
Chile	22	-2	2	829	-57	-108	253	25	293	168
Colombia	-1	14	15	527	-5	22	106	-623	115	137
Ecuador							19	45	-19	222
Mexico	40	43	56	1,177	92	47	1,464	510	1,949	2,472
Peru	-3	4	7	515	-46	312	131	-197	-346	-5
Venezuela	-43	27	-150	2,715	1	197	73	-205	39	435

Source: U.S. Department of Commerce, *Survey of Current Business,* various August issues.

Notice that the total flows really stagnated during the 1980s, as a result of the debt crisis, but then began to surge in the early 1990s. Also note that Argentina and Mexico were the two largest gainers of FDI inflow in the early 1990s, though in the case of U.S. FDI alone, Brazil also experienced large gains in the past few years. Argentina attracted a large amount of European (and Chilean) FDI during its massive privatization program in the early 1990s, while Brazil has not gone through such a degree of economic opening. Brazil has attracted more U.S. company expansion in this period, rather than large-scale inflow from European or Asian companies.

Sectoral Distribution of FDI in Latin America

The industry sectoral breakdown of FDI is available only for U.S. firms, as shown in Figure 2.

Notice that U.S. direct investment has concentrated primarily in manufacturing sectors (especially chemicals, foods, and transportation equipment) in the 1980s and 1990s, while petroleum and mining were more important in the 1950s and 1960s — up until the period of anti-foreign,

Table 4.
Total Private Direct Investment
Flows in Latin America, 1965-1994
(US$ millions)

Year	1965	1970	1975	1980	1981	1982	1983	1984	1985
Total LA	0	-37	107	4,865	7,056	5,511	2,832	2,825	3,899
Argentina	0	0	0	790	930	255	182	269	911
Brazil		0	0	1,545	2,317	2,551	1,374	1,555	1,282
Chile	0	-10	-6	171	362	384	132	67	62
Colombia	0	-2	-2	52	229	338	514	561	1,015
Ecuador	0	0	0	70	60	40	50	50	62
Mexico		-7	178	2,153	2,846	1,644	457	392	500
Peru	0	-7	0	29	128	46	37	-87	-1
Venezuela		-11	-63	55	184	253	86	18	68

Year	1986	1987	1988	1989	1990	1991	1992	1993	1994
Total LA	3,076	3,790	6,454	6,988	5,991	9,839	11,727	12,275	15,676
Argentina	576	-18	1,148	1,028	1,836	2,439	4,179	6,035	1,282
Brazil	180	79	2,269	744	236	-42	1,443	-292	931
Chile	56	97	109	1,279	582	400	321	410	870
Colombia	643	292	186	547	484	433	740	812	1,640
Ecuador	70	75	80	80	82	85	95	115	531
Mexico	1,515	3,212	2,596	3,174	2,634	4,762	4,393	4,901	7,980
Peru	20	32	46	59	41	-7	127	349	2,326
Venezuela	16	21	20	77	96	1,769	429	-55	116

Source: International Monetary Fund, *International Financial Statistics,* various issues.

inward-looking development that began in the 1970s. As well, investment in the financial sector has grown noticeably during the era of *apertura economica* in the early 1990s.

This overview of the industrial distribution of FDI obscures some of the interesting features that are country-specific. For example, the discovery of vast oil reserves in northern Colombia in the late 1980s has led to major investment in oil-related industries there — quite different from the general trend of focusing more on manufactures and services and less on raw materials in the region. Likewise, in Argentina with the number of major privatizations during the 1990-1993 period, foreign direct investment moved into nontraditional sectors such as telecommunications, electric power, water provision, and railroads — all of which were viewed traditionally as public utilities and usually operated by government agencies or government-owned companies.

Figure 2.
U.S. Foreign Direct Investment Position, 1950 - 1993
Latin America

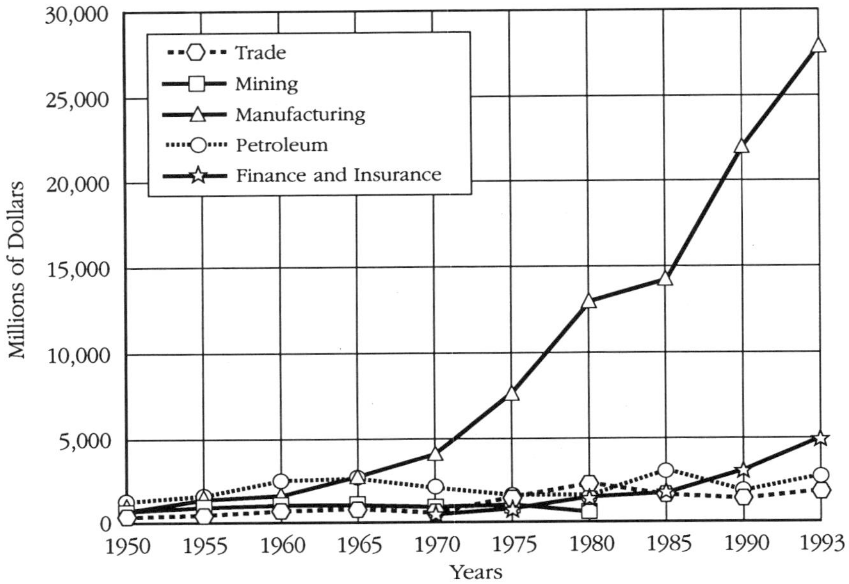

Source: U.S. Dept. of Commerce, *Survey of Current Business,* various issues.

Comparing FDI with Other Foreign Financing Sources

The trends in foreign direct investment into Latin America may be compared with those in portfolio investment, commercial bank lending, and official (government) lending. The picture from 1950 onward shows that official lending to government borrowers in Latin America initially dominated the foreign financial flows into the region. This situation changed in the 1970s, when commercial bank lending took off and more than tripled the value of official lending. The flow of foreign direct investment remained relatively small until the beginning of the 1990s, when it jumped dramatically from about $8.6 billion in 1990 to $14.4 billion in 1992. FDI and portfolio investment combined began to dominate foreign financing by the late 1980s. Figure 1 on page 136 depicted these changes in foreign finance to Latin America over the past half-century.

Bank lending has been the most volatile of the foreign financial flows into the region, while direct investment has shown a much more stable growth. Official government lending has tended to decline over time fairly consistently, both relatively and in absolute terms. Portfolio investment has been more stable than bank lending and generally higher than FDI flows through the years. Note that portfolio investment also has jumped substantially in the early 1990s in comparison with the trough during the debt crisis of 1982-1989. In sum, direct investment has never been the single leading source of foreign finance into Latin America, but its importance has grown substantially in the 1990s, and FDI along with portfolio investment are the primary engine of foreign funding today.

Departing from this comparison with other financing sources, the analysis below focuses on the causes of foreign direct investment in Latin America and on the relationship of that type of investment to local savings and investment.

Methodology

To explore the causes of FDI into Latin American countries, a macroeconomic model of such investment is constructed in the next section. This model is specified to explain the value of FDI flows (that is, capital outflows) into the region. This modeling is similar to that used to identify factors that contribute to aggregate FDI flows by Root and Ahmed (1979), Grosse and Trevino (1996), and others.

The model is specified to explain FDI into all the Latin American countries for which data were available, using a pooled sample of countries over time. Macroeconomic data are taken from World Bank and IMF publications to measure the factors in question. The intent in this portion of the analysis is to identify factors that are common across countries in producing FDI inflows.

A second modeling process was followed to explore the question of how direct investment contributes to capital formation in the Latin American region. The model compares the growth of capital formation (minus FDI) with the growth of FDI in Latin America; a positive correlation would imply that FDI contributes to domestic capital formation, where a negative correlation would imply that it replaces domestic capital formation.

A third modeling process is used to explore the relationship between FDI and domestic savings in Latin America. Similar to the question of FDI's impact on capital formation, it is important to know whether FDI represents foreign savings that replace domestic savings in Latin America, or if the two grow in parallel. The ideal would be for foreign direct investment to supplement domestic savings in generating funds for capital investment and GDP growth, regardless of the direction of growth/contraction of domestic savings. If FDI and savings move in tandem, then the implication is that periods of reduced savings in the region will result in reduced FDI as well, thus adding to the problem of finding finances for development.

The next section presents the analysis of determinants of FDI into Latin America and seeks to answer the question of what has caused the turnaround in FDI flows into Latin America in the 1990s. The following section presents both the savings and the domestic capital formation issues.

A Model of Aggregate FDI Flows

The determinants of foreign direct investment have been studied for many years in the international business literature (see, for example, Aharoni 1966; Vernon 1966; Kindleberger 1969; Ragazzi 1973; Froot 1993). These determinants may be analyzed on a company-specific basis, to explore the managerial reasons for perceived FDI patterns, or on an industry-specific basis, usually to examine both company and industry factors that may explain FDI patterns, or on an aggregate, country-level basis, to explore macroeconomic, macropolitical, and country-specific factors that contribute to FDI patterns. The present analysis is focused at the broadest level, at which macro and country-specific factors are considered.

The research question is what factors have contributed to the flow of FDI into Latin America in the past several decades. By isolating those factors, it may be possible to understand both the persistent influences on FDI activity and also the conditions that have changed in the 1990s and have led to a resurgence of FDI into the region.

A model of FDI was specified of the following form: FDI = f(economic and political factors). The factors that were considered are those that have been found to correlate with FDI in previous studies of direct investment around the world. They are the following:

size of the host country economy	(GDP in U.S. dollars)
growth rate of the host country economy	(percentage change in GDP)
international trade of the host country	(exports + imports in U.S. dollars)
local versus foreign rates of return	(local nominal deposit rate - annual exchange rate change - eurodollar deposit rate)
host country credit rating or country risk	(Frost & Sullivan investment risk rating)
host country inflation	(annual percent change in consumer price index)
host country fiscal balance	(converted to U.S. dollars)
host country foreign exchange reserves	(flow converted to U.S. dollars)
host country per capita income	(per capita GDP in U.S. dollars)
the international price of petroleum	(as quoted in *IFS*)

These factors were measured as shown in the listing, using data principally from the IMF publication, *International Financial Statistics*. They were used to construct a multivariate regression model, whose expected results are discussed here.

The size of the host country economy was expected to correlate strongly positively with FDI. This relationship has been found consistently in studies of FDI across countries and methodologies. The larger the target market, the more attractive it is to incoming FDI that is market-serving. (Of course, this ignores the FDI that may enter for offshore assembly (maquila) or offshore sourcing, both of which are important to multinational enterprise strategies in the 1990s, but both of which are small in relation to market-serving FDI in both industrial and emerging markets.)

The growth rate of the host country economy was expected to correlate positively with incoming FDI. This relationship should exist if faster-growing economies indeed do attract capital investment toward producing more goods and services to serve that market in the future. The significance of this variable in previous studies of FDI has been inconsistent. Often, after other factors have been taken into account, the growth rate proved insignificant in statistical models. The present model examines this relationship once more.

The level of international trade coming into and going out of the host country also is expected to be positively correlated with incoming FDI. This is because foreign firms are expected to serve the local market with both imports and FDI-plus-local production, and thus the two complement each other. Exports from the host country also may correlate with FDI in the cases of firms that use host country production to serve foreign markets, either through offshore sourcing or offshore assembly operations. In the present case, both total trade and imports alone were examined as factors contributing to FDI inflows.

Moving from measures of market size and growth, another type of factor that should relate to FDI is the relative rate of return available in the host country. This factor should correlate positively with FDI, meaning that higher local returns should attract greater amounts of foreign investment, of both portfolio and direct types. The relative rate of return was measured here as the local bank deposit rate, minus the realized devaluation of the local currency relative to the U.S. dollar for the period, minus the dollar deposit rate, LIBOR (London Inter-bank Offered Rate).

The attractiveness of the host country to FDI should also reflect the level of risk associated with the country. Various measures of country risk and political risk have been developed by analysts seeking to understand the risks facing bank lenders (for example, by *Euromoney* magazine and *Institutional Investor* magazine) and also the risks facing direct investors (for example, by Frost & Sullivan and by BERI, among others). Given that this study's concern is with investors in physical facilities, the investment risk measures are more appropriate, and the Frost & Sullivan measure in particular was chosen for its simplicity and consistency over time.[6] The expectation is that country risk will correlate negatively with FDI; the more risky the country, the less FDI anticipated.

Similar to the logic for country risk, many analysts have argued that the level of inflation in the host country should be negatively related to FDI flows. With higher or more unstable inflation, the host country environment should appear less attractive to potential investors and result in less FDI. Studies of this factor have been quite mixed in the literature. High or unstable rates of inflation as a proxy for country risk sometimes have been found to be significant as detractors of FDI, but generally they have proved insignificant in most models.

Alternatively, inflation may be used as a measure of costs such as wages in a country. FDI should be attracted to low-wage, low-cost environments, and thus inflation should have a negative correlation with FDI in the current context.

The government's ability to control fiscal policy (as monetary policy that contributes to inflation) may have an impact on FDI. The argument is that a positive fiscal balance, or a lower fiscal deficit, demonstrates better government control over the economy and hence better stability. This should attract FDI, other things being equal. Using fiscal balance as the measure, a more positive value should be correlated with a higher level of FDI.

The host country's availability of foreign exchange reserves also may have some impact on FDI. Greater levels of reserves lead to greater confidence by investors in the availability of funds for making their remittances and generally in gaining access to foreign currency when needed. Thus, the level of official foreign exchange reserves should correlate positively with FDI.

The per capita income of the host country may indicate the wealth of host country consumers and thus add to GDP as a measure of the country's purchasing power. From another perspective, using Linder's similarity of demand patterns, one would expect greater demand for imports by developing countries with higher levels of per capita income (more similar to industrial countries) and also greater demand for FDI for the same reason. Higher per capita income should thus correlate positively with FDI.

One unusual factor that is included here is the international price of oil. This factor contributed dramatically to the economies of Latin American countries during the 1970s, when the oil exporters gained enormously from the OPEC price hikes. Many non-oil exporters also gained from the generalized run-up of raw materials prices during that decade, which supported exporters of copper, bauxite, tin, and other minerals, metals, and even agricultural products that are the traditional export bases of Latin America. On this basis, one would expect that oil price increases would be associated with more rapid economic growth in Latin America. However, since the oil price hikes in the 1970s were accompanied by nationalizations of foreign oil companies, the relation to FDI may not be positive. In fact, oil price increases may be associated with greater bargaining power by Latin American governments and thus less willingness to allow FDI entry. Therefore, it may be expected that as oil prices rise, less FDI will enter the region, and as oil prices fall, governments will be more interested in attracting FDI, and the rate of FDI may increase.

Empirical Results

Results of testing the model are presented in Table 5 below. Because of the anticipation that some country-specific influences are not captured by the variables listed above, modeling was done using a least-squares, dummy variable framework, with country dummy variables. The test results were robust to the exclusion of country dummies, and the significance levels of the independent variables were improved generally when the country dummy variables were included.

Table 5.
Regression Results, Determinants of FDI

independent variable	coefficient	t-statistic signif. level
constant	-1130.83	0.000
GDP	0.01	0.000
growth rate of GDP	-1.11	0.013
per capita GDP	0.44	0.000
inflation	0.03	0.360
fiscal balance	0.03	0.001
official reserves	-0.01	0.889
interest rate	4.15	0.043
country risk	-5.23	0.058
oil price	-15.59	0.001
country dummy variables*		
adjusted R^2	0.87	
number of observations	169	

*All country dummy variables were significant at the .001 level, with positive signs.

A few of the intended independent variables were highly correlated. (See the correlation matrix in the Appendix.) For example, imports were correlated almost 90 percent with GDP, as was total trade. Since no simple means suggests itself for combining the two factors, the less-important one was dropped from the regression, namely the trade variables.

Table 5 shows that almost all of the factors that were anticipated to influence FDI into Latin American countries were statistically significant. Only inflation and official international reserves proved to be insignificant in the model. All of the signs of the variables were as expected, except for growth of GDP, which was unexpectedly negative. The regression model explained 87 percent of the variation of FDI into Latin American countries during the 1980-1993 period.

The question of what happened in the early 1990s to restimulate foreign direct investment into Latin America can be answered to some extent with the above findings. Namely, the variables that appear to contribute to FDI inflow into Latin America also should be those that, when they move positively, stimulate more FDI into the region (with the exception of country risk, which should move in the opposite direction). On inspection, it is clear that as GDP and per capita GDP began to increase markedly in the early 1990s, so also did the inflows of FDI. As perceptions of country risk improved (that is, as country risk lessened), FDI increased. In each of these cases, the improvements in underlying economic conditions appear to have contributed to investor confidence in Latin America and hence to increased FDI. This is consistent with the perceptions of country conditions as presented in the business literature such as *Business Latin America* and the *Lagniappe Newsletter*, each of which show increasingly positive outlooks for the region by the end of the 1980s and into the 1990s but generally negative outlooks from the onset of the external debt crisis in 1982.

The local rate of return was significantly positively correlated with FDI flows, indicating that FDI did more to take advantage of higher expected returns in Latin American countries. The fiscal balance of the government, interestingly, was strongly positively related to FDI flows. Apparently, during this period, the ability of a government to achieve a better balance of revenues and spending produced a greater degree of confidence and willingness to invest by direct investors.

Finally, the international price of oil was strongly negatively correlated with FDI flows into Latin America. This result is consistent with the experience of the 1970s, when oil price increases were correlated with faster economic growth in the region but also a lower willingness to allow foreign direct investment. During the 1980s, with declining oil prices (and declining GDP growth), the Latin American governments were more willing to permit and even encourage FDI inflows. During the 1990s, with fairly stable oil prices, other factors tended to drive FDI flows into the region.

The Relation of FDI to Domestic Savings and Investment

B asic issues of concern in this analysis include not only the reasons FDI takes place but also the ways in which FDI relates to domestic savings and investment. First, consider the relationship between FDI and capital investment from domestic sources. One would hope that inflows of FDI would add to national capital formation rather than replacing domestically owned with foreign-owned capital. Therefore, an explanation of domestic capital formation should include a positive correlation with FDI. This relationship was tested with a simple regression model, using data from 1980-1993. The regression was of the form: Domestic capital formation = $\alpha + \beta$ (FDI). Domestic capital formation was measured as total capital formation minus FDI. Empirical results were

Domestic Capital Formation =   0.75   +   1.97 (FDI)

(t=1.85)   (t=9.13)

and the regression's adjusted R^2 = 0.33. The relationship is positive and highly significant, indicating that FDI indeed does contribute to the development of domestic capital formation in Latin America (though it does not explain very much of the variation of domestic capital formation over time). This model is admittedly simplistic, but the intent is to demonstrate the direction and significance of the correlation.

It also should be noted that FDI is small relative to domestically generated capital formation. For all Latin America, FDI has averaged less than 2 percent of GDP and about 10 percent of domestic capital formation during the past two decades.[7] This fact should not be overstated, since FDI may be an important signal of confidence to investors in a country, and it may also attract other forms of financing such as portfolio investment and bank lending. Table 6 compares FDI as a percentage of total capital formation in selected Latin American countries.

Next, consider the relationship between FDI and domestic savings in Latin America. Does an increase in the rate of savings lead to an increase in FDI? This relationship also was examined through a simple bivariate regression. The relationship FDI = f(savings) produced a statistical model with almost no explanatory power and a highly insignificant coefficient on the savings term. Apparently, using this very elementary measure, the local savings rate does not influence the amount of FDI coming into the region.

This would be a favorable finding, if it is indeed supported by further more detailed analysis. That is, if the low savings rates in Latin American countries, relative especially to Asian emerging markets but also relative to industrial countries, do not detract from FDI inflows, then this savings weakness can be dealt with separate from the policy decisions related to FDI. On the other hand, it is quite possible that policies designed to build local savings, such as development of efficient local capital markets, would serve to attract more foreign direct investment as well.

Table 6.
Foreign Direct Investment as a Percentage
of Capital Formation

	Country			
Year	Argentina	Chile	Colombia	Mexico
1985	5.9	5.1	15.4	1.3
1986	3.1	11.4	10.7	6.3
1987	-0.1	24.2	4.3	12.0
1988	4.8	25.7	2.4	7.4
1989	8.6	25.3	7.3	6.9
1990	10.3	18.9	6.7	4.9
1991	8.8	11.4	6.5	7.4
1992	10.9	7.6	10.5	7.0
1993	13.3	13.8	8.7	n.a.

Source: Agosin 1995, 25.

Conclusion

Foreign direct investment in Latin America has proved to be an important engine of growth in the region during the first half of the 1990s. While not constituting a very large percentage of total capital formation in most countries in most years, FDI still plays an important role in the development of the economies of these countries. FDI correlates strongly with local capital investment and may be seen as an indicator of confidence in an economy that tends to draw with it more capital investment from local sources.

Foreign direct investment appears to be driven largely by market size in Latin America, as has been demonstrated repeatedly in the literature over the years. In addition, factors such as per capita income, the country's fiscal balance, and the available rate of return on investment all contribute positively to attract FDI. Perceived riskiness of the country and the price of oil showed strong negative impacts on the flow of FDI into Latin America.

Foreign direct investment is one of the sources of foreign savings that contributes importantly to economic development in the region. Government policies that encourage this activity will aid likewise in the development process, both by bringing in the foreign capital and by showing domestic investors that the private sector is being supported. The creation of a stable and favorable policy environment should not be overlooked as a factor that can assist in generating more capital investment and thus greater growth in the region.

Appendix.
Correlations of FDI Determinants

	GDP	GDPGROW	GDP/CAP	INFL	FISCBAL	RESERV	INTRATE	CTRYRSK	OILPRICE	FDI
GDP	1.00	0.06	0.55	-0.01	-0.25	0.39	-0.04	X.XX	0.07	X.XX
GDPGROW		1.00	0.07	0.40	-0.04	-0.02	0.74	X.XX	-0.02	X.XX
GDP/CAP			1.00	-0.11	0.01	0.23	-0.09	X.XX	0.51	X.XX
INFL				1.00	-0.04	0.01	0.51	X.XX	-0.04	X.XX
FISCBAL					1.00	-0.39	0.01	X.XX	0.02	X.XX
RESERV						1.00	-0.01	X.XX	0.13	X.XX
INTRATE							1.00	X.XX	-0.15	X.XX
CTRYRSK								1.00	X.XX	X.XX
OILPRICE									1.00	X.XX
FDI										1.00

Notes

1.   These waves of policy toward foreign firms are discussed in, for example, Agosin 1995.

2.   This view overstates the amount of FDI that is attributed to debt conversion and privatization programs. With a government policy environment of general economic opening and permission for foreign firms to operate locally in Latin American countries, much of the FDI in question may have occurred anyway, without the special incentives that were offered. Measuring this counterfactual alternative is, of course, not possible.

3.   Most of the direct investment at that time actually could be characterized as expatriate investment. That is, Spanish and Portuguese entrepreneurs moved to the Latin American countries and set up their own businesses that indeed received financial backing from supporters in the home country. But the new businesses were not typically extensions of firms from Europe; rather, they were new enterprises run by foreign nationals that were (partially) financed from abroad. See Grosse 1989, Chapter 1, for a description of direct investment activity in Latin America during the past 200 years.

4.   Capital investment in Latin America during the nineteenth century was much more commonly carried out through bond issues that were used by investment companies to finance mining or other ventures. Direct investment was less common, though nevertheless important as well.

5.   Cleona Lewis (1938) details this history.

6.   Frost & Sullivan changed its name to Political Risk Service, and the surveys are now done by that organization and using that name. The earlier name is used in the text because of its greater familiarity.

7.   These numbers are based on IMF data on FDI, GDP, and capital investment. See also Agosin 1995, Chapter 1.

References

Agosin, Manuel, ed. 1995. *Foreign Direct Investment in Latin America*. Washington, D.C.: Interamerican Development Bank.

Aharoni, Yair. 1966. *The Foreign Direct Investment Decision Process*. Boston: Harvard Business School Press.

Economist Intelligence Unit. *Business Latin America* (various issues).

Froot, Kenneth, ed. 1993. *Foreign Direct Investment*. Chicago: University of Chicago Press.

Grosse, Robert. 1989. *Multinationals in Latin America*. London: Routledge.

Grosse, Robert, and Len Trevino. 1996. "Foreign Direct Investment in the United States: An Analysis by Country of Origin." *Journal of International Business Studies*, Winter.

Kindleberger, Charles. 1969. *Foreign Direct Investment Abroad*. New Haven, Conn.: Yale University Press.

Latin American Information Services, *Lagniappe Letter*. New York: biweekly newsletter.

Lewis, Cleona. 1938. *America's Stake in International Investment*. Washington, D.C.: The Brookings Institution.

Linder, Stefan. 1961. *An Essay on Trade and Transformation*. New York: Wiley.

Ragazzi, Giorgio. 1973. "Theories of the Determinants of Direct Foreign Investment." *IMF Staff Papers* (July): 471-498.

Root, F., and A. Ahmed. 1979. "Empirical Determinants of Manufacturing Direct Foreign Investment in Developing Countries." *Economic Development and Cultural Change*, 751- 767.

United Nations. 1965. *External Financing in Latin America*. New York: United Nations.

Vernon, Raymond. 1966. "International Trade and International Production in the Product Cycle." *Quarterly Journal of Economics* (May).

Chapter 7

The Impact of Economic Opening on Savings in Latin America

José M. González-Eiras

Abstract

With the exhaustion of the import-substitution model after the debt crisis of 1982, a process of opening the economies of the region began in Latin America. This chapter seeks to determine how this process of reform affected levels of savings. It tests the Feldstein-Horioka hypothesis that the level of domestic savings determines the level of national investment. Thus, the chapter attempts to ascertain whether the relation between these two variables remains stable throughout the process of reform and, finally, whether opening affects the absolute levels of both savings and investment.

Introduction

During the 1980s, the economies of Latin America faced severe macro-economic disequilibria. The most direct consequences of these disequilibria were a low rate of gross domestic product (GDP) growth (1.2 percent a year for the region) and a negative trend in per capita GDP. Many factors combined to cause this outcome. From an internal perspective, it was clear that the development model organized around the domestic market — which had been instituted following World War II — had been exhausted. Among the external factors, the fall in international prices for primary goods — which made up the bulk of the region's exports — the excessive increase in international interest rates, and the proliferation of protectionism in the developed countries must be mentioned.

The extensive role of the state in productive activity and the severe distortions placed upon foreign trade in order to encourage internal production resulted in permanent disequilibrium in government accounts. These deficits were financed primarily with domestic savings. Toward the end of the 1970s, the greater availability of external financing allowed the region's governments to avoid having to make adjustments in their accounts, thereby accentuating disequilibrium.

The change in the international situation during 1982 had a twofold effect: On one hand, new credits became less available, and on the other, service payments on the existing debt rose as a result of international interest rate increases. This new reality forced Latin American countries to pursue — over the course of a number of years — a process of adjustment based on a restructuring of the public sector and an opening of their economies.

The purpose of this chapter is to determine how this process of economic opening influenced the overall level of savings in the Latin American economies. It assesses the validity of the Feldstein-Horioka hypothesis that the level of domestic savings is the determinant of national investment. Similarly, it seeks to establish whether the opening of the economy produced a change in the relationship between domestic savings and investment, as well as whether there was any parallel change in the average values of both variables.

Protectionism and its Effects on Levels of Savings and Investment

Since the 1940s, the evolution of the Latin American economies to a certain extent followed a common pattern marked by three clearly differentiated stages. The first stage began with the end of the Second World War, when staunch policies of import substitution were introduced. These relied on strong tariff and non-tariff protection. This phase ended only recently, toward the end of the 1970s, when an incipient process of external opening and financial deregulation spread throughout the region. The 1982 debt crisis put an abrupt end to this period before any important institutional reforms could be consolidated. In the short run, this crisis gave new life to protectionism. After the outbreak of the crisis, the need to reverse transfers of capital abroad — over $30 billion — left the countries of the region with no alternative but to reduce imports drastically.

As a result of the measures adopted, which included increases in import tariffs and quotas, the Latin American countries ended up with the highest levels of protection among all developing countries around the world. Finally, toward the end of the 1980s, most Latin American countries entered a third phase, during which they began to reverse these policies and open their economies to the rest of the world.

The duration and severity of protectionist policies distorted the external sector of the countries in the region. The principal effects of trade restrictions were to discourage the growth and diversification of exports in virtually every country. In his 1993 work for the World Bank, Sebastian Edwards maintains that the high degree of protection for manufacturing in Latin America caused a severe discrimination against exports, a misallocation of resources, unproductive investments, and a worsening distribution of income. Exports were dampened in two ways. On one hand, impediments to imports increased the cost of imported capital goods and inputs

Table 1.
Capital Inflows and Resource Transfers
(billions of U.S. dollars)

Year	Net Capital Inflows	Net Interest Payments	Net Resource Transfers
1978	26.2	10.2	16.0
1979	29.1	13.7	15.4
1980	32.0	18.9	13.1
1981	39.8	28.5	11.3
1982	20.1	38.8	-18.7
1983	2.9	34.5	-31.6
1984	10.4	37.3	-26.9
1985	3.0	35.3	-32.3
1986	9.9	32.6	-22.7
1987	15.4	31.4	-16.0

Source: United Nations Economic Commission for Latin America and the Caribbean (ECLAC), Economic Study of Latin America and the Caribbean, 1991.

used in producing exported commodities. Conversely, protectionist policies produced an overvalued real exchange rate, which diminished the international competitiveness of the domestic economies. It is interesting to note that regardless of the policy instrument used, the effect on the real exchange rate is the same. Whether taxes are imposed on exports or tariffs are placed on imports, the same effect on the real exchange rate occurs, a result that conforms with the Lerner symmetry theorem.

The process of economic opening in the Latin American countries was characterized by the following: 1) a lowering of the average level of tariff protection and 2) a reduction in non-tariff barriers. Furthermore, the dispersion in tariff levels also was lessened.

Grossman and Helpman (1990) maintain that economic opening has effects on technological progress and productivity, extends incentives to increase absolute levels of investment, and also increases the productivity of domestic savings. Within the same theoretical vein, Díaz Alejandro (1970) finds that the isolation of closed economies was responsible for the low productivity of savings levels. The existence of high tariffs and direct restrictions on capital entry results in quantitative differences in the availability of capital goods for a given volume of domestic savings. The existence of quotas and restrictions, which were widely used policy measures in Latin America, made it impossible to carry out a process of technological adaptation and to promote positive externalities through the

Table 2

Country	Average Tariff Protection*		Average Coverage of Non-Tariff Barriers**	
	1985	1991/1992	1985	1991/1992
Argentina	28.0	15.0	31.9	0.0
Bolivia	20.0	8.0	25.0	0.0
Brazil	80.0	21.1	35.3	10.0
Colombia	83.0	6.7	73.2	1.0
Costa Rica	92.0	16.0	0.8	0.0
Chile	36.0	11.0	10.1	0.0
Ecuador	50.0	18.0	59.3	n.d.
Mexico	34.0	4.0	12.7	20.0
Paraguay	71.7	16.0	9.9	0.0
Peru	64.0	15.0	53.4	0.0
Uruguay	32.0	17.0	44.1	5.0
Venezuela	30.0	17.0	44.1	5.0
Median	51.7	13.3	30.8	3.3
Dispersion (std.dev.)	24.0	4.8	21.8	6.1

n.d.: No data available.
* Mean total burden (tariff duties and semi-duties).
** Non-weighted.
Source: Edwards (1993) using World Bank database, Erzan, Refik, Kiroaki Kuwahara,
      Saratino Marchese and Rene Vossenar (1989).

incorporation of capital goods whose development costs had not been assumed by the reference country. Quotas and restrictions also blocked economies of scale in production, even in those countries with significant populations, such as Brazil and Mexico. Production in inefficient sectors implied a poor allocation of resources, as was demonstrated in the automotive, metallurgical, and steel industries.

With regard to the financial sector, Latin American countries for decades placed strict controls on financial activities. Interest rate ceilings and a discretionary allocation of credit were common practices. Under the influence of Keynesianism, which was pursued by many Latin American governments, it was widely believed that these instruments would accelerate capital accumulation and increase savings and the efficiency of investment, thereby stimulating the overall growth of the economy. The actual result was practically the opposite, since savings and financial intermediation were discouraged and the quality of private investment declined.

Toward the end of the 1970s, on the basis of the theoretical work of McKinnon (1973) and Shaw (1973), a number of Latin American economies began a process of economic opening and financial integration with the rest of the world. These policies were adopted to counteract the notable degree of isolation and control in which many countries had been immersed. The underlying idea was that economic opening and greater financial sophistication would have positive effects on growth by improving the allocation of capital, which would contribute to greater productivity and volume of investment. Nevertheless, in the early 1980s, many of these Latin American experiments with financial liberalization collapsed, leading to a general reevaluation of the theory.

De Gregorio and Guidotti (1994) have argued that the pursuit of financial liberalization in a relatively weak regulatory context contributed to increasing the fragility of the financial system. The result was an overexpansion of borrowing, entailing a subsequent massive intervention of the state as the backer of last resort.

After the debt crisis, a new attempt at economic opening was begun. This process proceeded gradually and assimilated the lessons of the early 1980s by providing for a strict regulatory framework to allow the financial system to sustain itself without the need for government intervention.

International Mobility of Capital and Savings

The debate on economic opening and its effect on the relationship between domestic savings and investment centers on two points: how the opening process affects absolute values of both variables and whether the relationship between one and the other remains stable. The latter issue brings up the problem of financing once again. Regarding this point, in a world with perfect mobility of capital, investment financing does not have to be supplied by domestic savings (Feldstein-Horioka 1980).

The central objective of this section is to provide a brief summary of the theories that fostered the study of the relation between domestic savings and investment. Subsequently, a similar analysis will be made with data on the Latin American economies to test whether the tendencies found among the Organization for Economic Cooperation and Development (OECD) countries also hold true for Latin American countries.

Toward the beginning of the 1980s, an intellectual current began to take shape within economic theory that sought to study the link between domestic investment and the level of domestic savings in the most developed countries. Works by North American economists Martin Feldstein and Charles Horioka were the precursors for this line of thinking.

Both maintained that capital flows among countries would equalize the net rate of return on taxes. Using data on the yield on short-term bonds, they demonstrated that capital movements occurred sufficiently rapidly to compensate for differences in yields. Nevertheless, both authors retained a certain skepticism regarding the arbitrage of long-term interest rates: Insofar as the risk in different countries and currencies is not perfectly correlated, individual and corporate investors have to choose portfolios in which the expected returns are not identical. Once some investors perceive that the risks for long-term investments are too high, there may coexist situations in which short-term differentials are balanced out, but there is no arbitrage of long-term interest rates. Similarly, from a domestic perspective, restrictions on capital exports, along with certain institutional rigidities, would cause domestic savings to remain in their country of origin.

The statistical estimates of the authors indicate that most of the marginal change in savings remained in the domestic markets. This result seriously called into question the assumption of perfect mobility in capital markets. Feldstein and Horioka's simplest test of perfect capital mobility in international markets consisted of a simple regression model in which the dependent variable was the rate of investment (I), measured as a percentage of the product (Y), and the independent variable was the ratio of savings (S) to level of income:

(1) $(I/Y)_i = \alpha + \beta(S/Y)_i + E_i$

In a world with perfect capital mobility, there should not be a correlation between domestic savings and domestic investment since savings in each country should respond to investment possibilities in any part of the world.

Nevertheless, the results of this model contradicted the hypothesis of perfect mobility of capital in international markets. For the countries studied during the years 1960-1974, and in successive five-year periods, β reached values around 0.9. Although there were important capital flows during this period, the determinants of these flows should be sought in factors other than domestic savings. According to these authors, a good part of direct investment in external markets can be explained by market strategies, the exploitation of knowledge associated with specific production processes, and efforts to avoid tariff restrictions, rather than a blind pursuit of profits.

An alternative explanation of the strong correlation was formulated by Dooley, Frankel, and Mathieson (1987), who tried to give a different interpretation to the association of investment and domestic savings. They argued that high values of β did not necessarily challenge the assumption of perfect mobility of capital. They called into question the integration of national markets in capital assets. The degree of substitutability of capital assets across different countries is not as high as in the different bond markets. Therefore, it should be expected that real investment necessarily must be financed through domestic savings.

Dooley, Frankel, and Mathieson also tried to determine whether the relation between investment and domestic savings might be influenced by a third variable, such as the degree of openness of an economy. As a measure of openness, they took the volume of external trade as a ratio of the product and postulated that in an economy open to flows of international trade, there would be a much weaker correlation between savings and investment.

$$(2)\ (I/Y)_i = \alpha + \beta(S/Y)_i + t(X+M)/Y + e$$

The regression results led these authors to conclude that there was not a statistically significant, linear relationship between the level of investment and the degree of openness of the economy, nor did they find variation in the estimates of ß.

Within this theoretical framework, this work estimates econometric regression equations for the 12 largest (measured in terms of GDP) Latin American countries. The data on savings, investment, and domestic product are drawn from the Economic Commission on Latin America's (ECLA) statistical annuals, whereas the data on trade and fiscal deficits are from the International Monetary Fund's (IMF) *International Financial Statistics*.

To analyze the estimated results for equation (1), the countries of the area were divided into three groups according to the longevity of their reform processes: Group 1 corresponds to the countries that first embarked upon reform — Chile, Mexico, and Bolivia; Group 2 is made up of recent reformers — Costa Rica and Uruguay; and Group 3 brings together the most recent reformers — the seven remaining countries. The period of reference for these series spans the years 1975-1993. Estimated coefficients are reported, and t-statistics for each are provided in parentheses.

Table 3.
Regression I - Response of the Level of Domestic Investment to the Rate of Domestic Savings 1975-1993

Group	α	ß	r^2	Durbin-Watson Test
I	0.14	0.17	0.04	1.02**
	(2.99)	(0.62*)		
II	0.12	0.29	0.05	1.10**
	(2.23)	(0.79*)		
III	0.11	0.33	0.20	0.85**
	(2.33)	(1.63*)		

* Statistically insignificant at the .05 level.
** With a confidence level of 95 percent, the hypothesis that the error terms are not autocorrelated can be rejected.

As can be seen from the results, the regression estimates suffer from serious problems of autocorrelation in the error terms, thereby distorting the results. Nevertheless, even though the ß are not statistically significant, the signs are in the expected direction, and it is interesting to note that in the group of countries that embarked upon reform earliest, there appears to be a weaker relationship between savings and domestic investment. That the magnitude of the coefficients is inversely related to the longevity of the reform process might be linked in part to the smaller risk premium faced by the earlier countries, which might have granted them a greater degree of independence in financing specific investment projects. Some authors (Bayoumi 1989), in contrast to the original Feldstein-Horioka work, use as variables the changes in the savings-product and investment-product ratios, but the estimates obtained with these variables for both the OECD and Latin American countries do not differ substantially from the original model.

To overcome the autocorrelation problem, three time lags for investment were incorporated into the original equation, thereby constructing an auto-regressive process.

$$(3)\ (I/Y) = \alpha + \text{ß}(S/Y) + Sd_i(I/Y)_{t-i}\ i=1,2$$

The following results were obtained for the same period of analysis using the same classification by longevity of the reform process:

Table 4.
Regression II - Response of the Level of Domestic Investment to the Rate of Domestic Savings and Lagged Investment (1975-1993)

Group	α	ß	d_1	d_2	r^2 corr.
I	0.14	0.17	0.26	-0.09	0.49
	(2.78*)	(2.42*)	(2.87*)	(-1.24*)	
II	0.07	0.21	0.48	0.11	0.79
	(3.29*)	(2.31*)	(2.76*)	(2.53*)	
III	0.05	0.34	0.41	-0.20	0.72
	(2.79*)	(2.23*)	(2.93*)	(-1.32*)	

* Statistically significant at a 95 percent confidence interval.

The regression results more than speak for themselves. Once levels of investment in recent periods are included as explanatory values, there is a decrease in the estimated coefficients of the relationship between domestic savings and domestic investment. The relationship between both variables is much weaker than that originally estimated for the OECD countries by Feldstein and Horioka. All of the ß are individually statistically significant, as are the coefficients for the first investment lag variable. The estimates for the other two lags are only statistically significant for the second group of countries. Using a measure of confidence of the adjustment corrected for the number of independent variables in the model, improvement is observed. The estimated model explains between 49 and 79 percent of the total variance.

It is interesting to note that on average a one-unit increase in savings positively affects investment by only approximately 0.2 units. This might be explained by assuming that Latin America faces a perfect capital market. However, the explanation of capital movements should not be sought in an equalization of returns but in massive flights of capital and inflows of funds by residents in response to the volatility of local economic policies. In this sense, massive capital flight occurred toward the beginning of the 1980s, whereas since the early 1990s, there has been a process of capital repatriation.

Among the problems related to financing, the following tests whether statistically significant results are attained when the external sector is incorporated into the original regression model amplified with lagged investment variables. In this instance, all the countries are considered together, without disaggregating according to level of openness.

Table 5.
Regression III – Response of the Level of Domestic Investment to the Rate of Domestic Savings, Lagged Investment, and the Degree of Opening (1975-1993)

α	ß	d_1	d_2	ET
0.09	0.24	0.31	-0.13	0.17
(2.19*)	(2.17*)	(2.14*)	(-1.71*)	(1.47*)

* Statistically significant at a 95 percent confidence interval.

Even though the economic opening variable is not statistically significant within any of the groups, the coefficient for the volume of external trade (ET) is in the expected direction for all three groups. This indicates that, controlling for domestic savings, greater levels of opening give rise to even further increases in domestic investment.

Using data for a number of countries in the region, a recursive process was carried out to determine whether economic opening has resulted in changes in the relation between savings and investment. Possibly because these events are so recent, in statistical terms it could not be concluded that there have been structural changes.

Independent of this analysis of the problem of financing, it is important to report trends in absolute levels of savings and investment. Traditionally, Latin America has had a low rate of domestic savings. In 1980, the gross domestic savings reached, on average, 20.4 percent of the GDP of the region, only 2 percent greater than in 1970. During the same period, investment stood around 24 percent of GDP, with the difference between domestic investment and savings covered by the availability of foreign resources.

This negative differential between domestic savings and investment that was a constant after the Second World War (particularly during the period between 1960 and 1980) reveals incentive distortions in the economy. According to a World Bank report (1992), "the worst aspect was that for decades savings — both internal and external — were used to finance projects of uncertain profitability."

As mentioned previously, strong distortions in international trade and the finance sector had a negative impact on the allocation of resources, the efficiency of investment, and the growth of productivity.

The low level of domestic savings should not only be attributed to private sector behavior. The domestic savings of a country can be broken down into two sources: private sector savings and public sector savings. If the state maintains a policy of imbalance in its fiscal accounts, then these deficits will be compensated by private domestic savings and financing from the rest of the world.

The use of the identity savings-investment, or the budgetary restriction of the economy as a whole, may be a useful analytical guide:

(Budget Deficit)=(Private Savings – Private Investment) +

(Current Account Deficit)

There are four ways that a state can finance the public sector deficit: domestic indebtedness, the utilization of the country's foreign exchange reserves, external indebtedness, and expansion of the money supply. The abuse of these sources of financing causes specific macroeconomic imbalances. The expansion of the quantity of money may be associated with inflationary phenomena; the utilization of the stock of foreign exchange reserves may result in exchange crises; foreign indebtedness may lead to a crisis of the external debt; and finally, domestic indebtedness is associated with high real interest rates and, possibly, as a result of servicing the public debt, an explosive dynamic of further indebtedness.

Prior to the process of economic opening and state reform, every government in the region used relatively indiscriminately all four types of financing. External financing is limited by the degree of trust the rest of the world confers upon the receiving country. This trust is determined basically by the evolution of the current account. Throughout the 1980s, the current accounts of the Latin American countries ran deficits at about $16 billion per year. Given the magnitude of this figure, it is difficult to imagine that the rest of the world could continue to finance the level of internal consumption in the domestic economies, which was stimulated by the sharp disequilibrium between public sector income and expenditures. This situation meant that private sector actors had to finance the public sector, thereby disassociating absolute levels of domestic savings from those of investment. Similarly, all the macroeconomic imbalances previously mentioned as linked to alternative means of financing public deficits appeared, giving rise to the debt crisis that emerged in 1982 and the severe monetary imbalances in the following years until the first attempts at reform were implemented.

Two periods are defined in order to consider how trends in savings and investment evolved prior to and after the reform process. The first period spans the years 1980-1985, and the second covers the years 1989-1993. Though this breakdown may at first appear arbitrary, intuitively it makes sense, since it omits the years 1986-1988 during which all countries in the region began to implement adjustments and data on national accounts were severely biased.

Table 6.
Levels of Domestic Savings and Investment in Latin America Before and After Reform

	Before Reform (1980-1985)		After Reform (1989-1993)	
	Savings	Investment	Savings	Investment
Group I	18.96	18.94	20.69	18.91
Group II	17.13	18.57	18.24	16.45
Group III	21.95	22.09	19.63	18.17

After the process of opening and public sector reform, as expected, an increase in domestic savings for the countries that first implemented reforms (Groups I + II) was observed. This increase in savings is primarily a result of the correction of fiscal disequilibria. The late reformers (Group III), on the other hand, are going against the current, with the level of savings dropping 2 percent of GDP after reform. This drop may be associated with the historical proximity of the reform process.

The efficiency of savings appears to have increased in all countries, although in the early reformers, this increase was also accompanied by a rise in the absolute levels of savings. As a consequence of the years of severe macroeconomic disequilibria (1982-1987), investment fell drastically. This contraction was due to an insufficient inflow of capital and the fall in the levels of public investment. In some countries, this decline in public investment was so severe that they were unable even to maintain their existing infrastructure. Even though there has been considerable recovery over the past years, in most countries investment has not reached the level that preceded the crisis, even in those cases where processes of privatization created strong incentives for increasing both domestic and external savings.

Conclusion

To test the validity of the Feldstein and Horioka hypothesis, a simple regression model associating levels of savings and investment was used, with countries grouped according to the longevity of the reform process in each country. The estimated ß coefficients were not statistically significant. The Durbin-Watson test confirmed autocorrelation in the error terms. The problem of autocorrelation was overcome by incorporating three investment lag variables as independent variables into the original equation. This correction not only considerably raised the explanatory power of the regression, but it also produced ß coefficients that were statistically significant at a 95 percent confidence level.

The analysis of the ß in this last case reveals a significant finding: The mean value for the region is very low, approximately 20 percent. Although, as economic theory explains, this level results from the exchange of capital with the rest of the world, it would be incorrect to infer that Latin America faces a perfect, international capital market.

Feldstein and Horioka explain capital flows among countries in terms of an equalization of expected returns, whereas in the Latin American cases, the result is a process of massive capital flight and entry by residents in response to the high volatility of economic policies in the region.

Finally, it should be noted that, as a result of the proximity of the opening process in the region, there are insufficient data to determine whether there has been a structural change in the relationship between savings and investment. This difficulty is exacerbated by the inclusion of investment lags as an explanatory variable.

They also tried to determine the effect of economic opening upon absolute levels of savings and investment. This was done by grouping the countries in the same manner as for the econometric regressions and averaging the data within two periods, 1980-1985 and 1989-1993. Thus, the years 1986-1988 are left aside; during these years, all the countries of the region began, with varying intensity, to reform their economies.

The results show a considerable recuperation in levels of savings in those countries that began their reform processes earliest. On the other hand, a two percentage point drop in savings in the group of late reformers was observed. Concurrently, due to the severe macroeconomic disequilibrium that arose throughout the 1980s, a decline was observed in the levels of investments. With the opening and consequent improvement in efficiency, this trend begins to turn around, especially in the first reformers. Nevertheless, investment has not yet recovered to pre-crisis levels.

In regards to the impact of financial sector reform upon savings, it can be said that the higher real interest rates, which resulted from deregulation of this sector, will translate into portfolio adjustments but not necessarily to an increase in total savings. This effect may happen because when an economy is in equilibrium, an increase in interest rates produces two contrary effects: An intertemporal substitution takes place, which lowers consumption and increases domestic savings, and there is a wealth effect that tends to reduce savings.

The final result depends on which of the two forces dominates. According to the results in this essay, during an initial moment, between economic opening and financial deregulation, the income effect is predominant and lowers the level of savings, but after some time passes, the substitution effect takes over, and domestic savings increase.

References

Bayoumi, T. 1989. "Saving-Investment Correlations: Immobile Capital, Government Policy or Endogenous Behavior?" *Working Paper* No. 88, International Monetary Fund.

De Gregorio, J., and P. Guipotti. 1994. *Financial Development and Economic Growth*. Research Dept., Working paper, International Monetary Fund.

Díaz Alejandro, C. 1970. *Essays on the Economic History of the Argentine Republic*. New Haven, Conn.: Yale University Press.

Dooley, M., J. Frankel, and D. Mathieson. 1987. "International Capital Mobility: What do Saving-Investment Correlations Tell Us?" *Staff Papers* 31. International Monetary Fund.

Edwards, S. 1993. *América Latina y el Caribe. Diez Años Después de la Crisis de la Deuda*. World Bank, Oficina Regional de América Latina y el Caribe.

Edwards, S. 1995. *Crisis and Reform in Latin America: From Despair to Hope*. New York: Oxford University Press.

Erzan, Refik, Kiroaki Kuwahara, Saratino Marchese, and Rene Vussenar. 1989. "The Profile of Protection in Developing Countries." *UNCTAD Review* 1 (1).

Feldstein, M. 1983. "Domestic Saving and International Capital Movements in the Long Run and the Short Run." *European Economic Review* 21, 129-151.

Feldstein, M., and C. Horioka. 1980. "Domestic Saving and International Capital Flows." *Economic Journal* 90, 314-329.

Fischer, S., and W. Easterly. 1990. "The Economics of the Government Budget Constraint." *The World Bank Research Observer* 5.

Grossman, G., and E. Helpman. 1990. "Comparative Advantage and Long Run Growth." *American Economic Review* 80, 796-815.

McKinnon, R. 1973. *Money and Capital in Economic Development*. Washington, D.C.: The Brookings Institution.

Shaw, E. 1973. *Financial Deepening in Economic Development*. New York: Oxford University Press.

Chapter 8

Building and Channeling Savings in Latin America: Conclusions

Robert Grosse

The set of papers in this volume has described a wide range of aspects of savings in Latin America during the past two decades and especially during the period of *apertura economica* in the 1990s. The most striking finding of the analyses is that, while high output growth rates recently have resumed throughout the region, high domestic savings rates have not. In many countries, domestic savings (both national and private) have fallen since the mid-1980s. More than ever before, Latin American countries save a smaller fraction of their output than other newly industrializing countries.

It is difficult to interpret this observation. Low savings now may indicate low growth in the future. In accord with traditional models of economic growth, there is strong presumption that higher savings funds capital formation and hence helps foster growth. Moreover, some believe in a "virtuous circle": Increased growth helps countries to save more.[1]

However, another widely accepted point of view, the permanent income hypothesis (PIH), has some very different implications for the savings/growth relationship. If an economy's residents (individually and in the aggregate) correctly perceive future increases (decreases) in output growth, they decrease (increase) savings. This reflects a key idea of the PIH, namely that people use savings to smooth consumption over time.[2] Thus, higher rates of output growth may be observed with *lower* savings rates.

According to Evan Tanner, there has been a negative correlation between *lagged* savings and growth in Latin America over the period 1960-1993. This observation supports the PIH. If Latin Americans are behaving now as in the past, they simply are acting according to the PIH, consuming out of future income. Also, the data indicate a high offset between private and public savings, suggesting that while governments successfully may cut deficits, they are less effective in promoting national savings.

Current low national savings rates may simply reflect optimism about future economic growth. If this optimism is correct and the Latin American countries succeed in propelling their economies into sustained growth along the lines followed by their Asian counterparts during the 1970s and 1980s, then this decline in current savings will have been justified by higher incomes.

The ultimate outcome of this process remains to be seen. Apart from Mexico and Argentina, there appears to be little faltering of growth rates in Latin America after five years of economic opening. So there is clearly reason to anticipate that future incomes will be higher and that lower savings today will not be penalized in the future.

Nonetheless, low savings in Latin America still may pose a problem. A major difference between the Latin American and the Asian newly industrializing countries is still that the savings rate in Latin America is similar to that of the United States (under 20 percent of GDP), while in Asia savings rates have been almost double that for two decades. This disparity may very well imply, according to recent growth models (for example, Mankiw, Roemer, and Weil 1992), a slower rate of long-term growth in Latin America, especially as foreign savings start to enter the region more slowly and domestic savings are required to take up more of the load of financing capital investment. According to the logic of portfolio diversification, once foreign investors and lenders have distributed their portfolios to include Latin American assets that formerly were prohibited by legal barriers, inflows should ultimately balance outflows. Even though this higher level of foreign savings that enters the region through direct and portfolio investment will support more capital formation than previously, still the growth rate cannot be sustained without generating more savings from somewhere — presumably from domestic savers. This situation may arrive as early as the end of the 1990s, but it is still several years away.

Of course, reliance on foreign savings may have implications for stability in the short run. As a result of factors out of a country's control, foreign capital can exit quickly, often leaving a country's banking system with liquidity problems. A good example of this is Argentina during 1995. As a consequence of the Mexican crisis (known popularly as the *Tequila Effect*), large and rapid capital outflows from Argentina caused severe liquidity problems at home. Ultimately, the government resorted to borrowing from the International Monetary Fund. The policy lesson from Argentina favors precautionary measures on foreign capital, such as higher reserve requirements or a transactions tax on capital inflows or outflows. Such measures should not discourage capital movements, but they should be high enough to provide sufficient insurance against turbulence in world capital markets.

Regarding institutional characteristics of savings and investment in Latin America, new mechanisms have recently and rapidly appeared. The development of domestic securities markets that actively trade stock shares and not just government bonds is a new phenomenon that promises to continue to attract domestic and foreign investors into holding shares of Latin American companies. The ability of Latin American issuers to capture investment through issue of American Depository Receipts in New York and newly developed Global Depository Receipts in London has appeared for the first time in the early 1990s. This mechanism has enabled dozens of firms to attract new capital for their expansion. Jaramillo and Curci describe how ADRs have boosted the borrowing capabilities of Colombian firms in recent years. Financial innovations such as commercial paper, futures contracts, and collateralized bonds have become common throughout Latin America and have enabled financial managers to hedge their risks, assure needed liquidity, and mobilize their savings to an unexpectedly rapid and extensive degree.

Erik Haindl analyzed one of the most noted regulatory innovations in the region, the privatization and deregulation of pension funds. Chile began this process in 1980 and immediately created a set of new financial institutions (that is, the pension fund management companies). Almost as quickly, the Chilean system developed a huge new demand for long-term investment opportunities, as the pension funds were permitted to expand their investments beyond government bonds and bank deposits into corporate issues and other assets, domestic and foreign. By allowing pension funds to be managed on a for-profit basis and by allowing them to invest in a much wider array of financial instruments, Chile's government was able dramatically to stimulate the mobilization of savings into investment. That process attracted foreign as well as domestic savings into the Chilean financial system.

Clarice Pechman analyzed the foreign financing alternatives available to Brazil in the 1990s. She found, not surprisingly, that bank loans constituted the largest part of the financing portfolio. In addition, innovations such as American Depository Receipts, commercial paper, and eurobonds enabled Brazilian firms to obtain significant foreign financing.

Her paper then explored the relations of domestic savings with foreign savings and both with the booms and busts of Brazilian economic growth since 1980. She found that government dis-saving accompanied the decline into deep recession at the beginning of the debt crisis and that domestic private sector savings and foreign savings did not grow enough to offset this burden. Then at the end of the 1980s and into the 1990s, domestic savings have tended to decline somewhat, while foreign savings coming into Brazil have risen. The net result is an overall decline in Brazil's savings rate relative to national income, just as other writers found for other countries and for Latin America as a whole. Pechman's analysis does not resolve the issue, but it brings a closer understanding of the Brazilian version of it.

Robert Grosse looked at the phenomenon of foreign direct investment, another vehicle for bringing foreign savings into Latin America. This investment has grown rapidly during the 1990s, though it remains behind portfolio investment and bank lending as a source of foreign capital in the mid-1990s. Foreign direct investment is a key part of total foreign financing both for its size and for its clear links to domestic investment. When foreign direct investment grows in the region, so also does domestic capital formation. There may well be a demonstration effect: As well-known companies invest in the region, this will attract additional foreign competitors to enter the market as well. Foreign direct investment tends to follow market size and development, but it pulls along with it additional investment.[3]

Foreign direct investment in Latin America historically has been dominated by U.S. firms since the turn of the last century, and earlier by British firms. As the twenty-first century approaches, U.S. firms still will be seen to lead those from other countries, but the percentage of U.S. FDI in the total is now and will remain well less than one-half.

Very surprisingly, FDI into Latin America showed no relationship to domestic savings in the region. Thus, with respect to savings, FDI must be seen as a channel for foreign savings to enter Latin America rather than a driving force behind domestic investment there.

Finally, José Maria González-Eiras explored specifically the past few years of economic opening in the region and tried to establish links between the timing of countries' entry into the process of opening and their rates of economic growth. He found that the countries that had entered into the apertura economica sooner were experiencing greater rates of growth during the early 1990s than their later counterparts. He also found that the savings rates of countries that began the process of apertura earlier are higher than the other Latin American countries. This finding might provide a basis for anticipating an increase in savings in the future for the other countries — similar to the result expected by Tanner following the permanent income hypothesis.

All in all, there seem to be reasons to expect an increase in the aggregate savings rate in Latin America in the future. This does not mean that these countries will match their Asian rivals in this regard, but rather that there is hope to see a higher rate of savings (and thus sustainable investment) in Latin America in the near future. It will be very interesting to see how development does progress in Latin America over the few remaining years of this century. The foundation is set for continued growth based on the free market model. The higher level of economic integration that prevails today throughout the world also gives hope to expect that the positive growth process will continue in Latin America.

Notes

1. For recent empirical evidence regarding savings and growth, see Mankiw, Romer, and Weil 1992.

2. For a formal statement of this point of view, see Campbell 1987 and Campbell and Deaton 1989.

3. Balasubramanyam and Sapsford (1996) demonstrate that FDI contributes significantly to economic growth in less-developed countries and contributes more significantly in countries that follow export-promotion rather than import-substitution economic policies.

References

Balasubramanyam, V.N., M. Salisu, and David Sapsford. 1996. "Foreign Direct Investment and Growth in EP and IS Countries." *The Economic Journal* (January): 92-105.

Campbell, J.Y. 1987. "Does Saving Anticipate Labor Income? An Alternative Test of the Permanent Income Hypothesis." *Econometrica* 55: 1249-1273.

Campbell, J.Y., and A. Deaton. 1989. "Why is Consumption So Smooth?" *Review of Economic Studies* 56: 357-374.

Mankiw, N.G., David Roemer, and David Weil. 1992. "A Contribution to the Empirics of Economic Growth." *Quarterly Journal of Economics* 107 (May): 407-437.

Contributors

Robert Grosse, project coordinator, is Professor of International Business at Thunderbird, The American Graduate School of International Management. He currently serves as Director of Research for Thunderbird. He has written extensively about foreign direct investment, particularly in Latin America. He has also written about the Latin American debt crisis of the 1980s and its aftermath.

Evan Tanner is Associate Professor of Economics at Thunderbird, The American Graduate School of International Management. He has written articles about savings patterns in various countries, and he works generally on the macroeconomics of Latin America.

Roberto Curci is currently a doctoral student in International Business Administration at the University of Texas Pan American. He was a professor at ICESI in Cali, Colombia, when this project was carried out. His research and business interests focus on international finance and capital markets in Latin America.

Fernando Jaramillo is Professor of Finance at ICESI (Instituto Colombiano de Estudios Superiores de INCOLDA) in Cali, Colombia, and also at CEIPA in Colombia. He has written about corporate financing strategies and about financial systems and capital markets.

Clarice Pechman is Executive Director of ANECC, the Brazilian Association of Currency Dealers, and Member of the Board of FICC — The Interamerican Federation of Currency Dealers. She has written extensively about foreign currency regimes, particularly in the case of Brazil.

Erik Haindl is Professor of Economics and Director of the Institute of Economics at the Universidad Gabriela Mistral in Santiago, Chile. He is also a member of the panel of fiscal experts of the IMF. He has written several articles about the Chilean economy as well as about most Latin American countries.

José María González-Eiras is Professor and Director of the Masters in Business Administration program at the Universidad del Salvador in Buenos Aires, Argentina. He is also a private consultant in international trade and international relations. He has written articles and other studies on economic and financial subjects such as social security, education, and others.

Index

New York Stock Exchange. *See NYSE*
NFP (net foreign factor payments) 125, 126, 127, 128
Nicaragua 138
non-sponsored ADRs. *See ADRs*
Norway 103
NYSE (New York Stock Exchange) 89, 90, 91, 94, 95, 96, 97, 98, 110

O

OECD (Organization for Economic Cooperation and Development) 159, 162
offshore assembly 145
OLS (ordinary least squares) 126, 127
Organization for Economic Cooperation and Development. *See OECD*
OTC (over-the-counter) 47, 48, 87, 88, 89, 92, 93, 94
over-the-counter. *See OTC*

P

Panama 15, 29, 138
Paraguay 10, 15, 29, 77, 81, 138, 158
pension system (pension fund) 7, 8, 113, 114, 115, 119, 121, 132
  fully funded 6, 7, 113, 114, 117, 120
  pay-as-you-go 6, 7, 113, 114, 115, 116, 117, 119, 120, 132
  reform 113, 114, 115, 116, 117, 119, 120, 130, 131, 134
permanent income hypothesis. *See PIH*
Persian Gulf War 54
Peru 8, 10, 14, 15, 17, 20, 29, 30, 137, 138, 140, 141, 158
PIH (permanent income hypothesis) 3, 13, 14, 18, 30, 125, 128, 129, 169, 172
Plano Real 26

PORTAL (Private Offerings, Resales, and Trading through Automated Linkages) 92
portfolio investment 2, 8, 11, 44, 60, 135, 136, 137, 142, 143, 149, 170, 171
private pension funds. *See AFPs*
private savings. *See Sp*
private sector 1, 3, 7, 13, 14, 17, 19, 22, 27, 31, 33, 34, 35, 36, 37, 55, 62, 71, 77, 119, 124, 136, 150, 164, 171
privatization 3, 5, 6, 8, 14, 63, 65, 76, 77, 97, 100, 119, 137, 140, 141, 152, 165, 171
  programs 3, 63, 106, 152
PT (Workers Party) 67
public sector 1, 3, 14, 17, 19, 22, 24, 27, 30, 41, 62, 71, 83, 119, 131, 132, 156, 164, 165

Q

QIBs (qualified institutional buyers) 92
qualified institutional buyers. *See QIBs*

R

Real Plan 30, 59, 63, 64, 65, 66, 73, 74, 76
reference rate. *See TR*
REH (Ricardian Equivalence Hypothesis) 24, 31
REP (Ricardian Equivalence Proposition) 19
Resolution 63 50, 52, 56, 76
Ricardian equivalence 19, 24, 30, 34, 129, 132
Ricardian Equivalence Hypothesis. *See REH*
Ricardian Equivalence Proposition. *See REP*
Rule 144A 92, 97, 103, 104, 106, 108

Production Notes

This book was printed on 60 lb. Glatfelter Natural text stock with a 10 point C1S cover.

The text of this book was set in Garamond by the North-South Center Press, using Pagemaker 6.0, on a Macintosh PowerPC 8500/120 computer. It was designed and formatted by Susan Kay Holler. The index was created by Mary M. Mapes.

The cover was created by Susan Kay Holler, using Macromedia Freehand 5.0.

The book was edited by Jayne M. Weisblatt.

This publication was printed by Thomson Shore of Dexter, Michigan, U.S.A.

DATE DUE

DEC 2 2 1999